# What ELSE Your Boss Never Told You

More Timely Tips
For New Managers

Gary Winters

## What Readers Are Saying...

Well, Gary is at it again. *What ELSE Your Boss Never Told You* is just as valuable as the rest of his collection of management books that have made me a better manager, and more importantly, a better person. His easy-to-read style and wonderful, relevant stories makes you feel that you are sitting right next to him exploring the art of management in person. A must read, again and again, if you want to be better today than yesterday.

Craig Bronzan<br>
Retired Parks and Recreation Director<br>
Principal, Bronzan Consulting

I think every student in the Masters program Engineering Management at Case Western Reserve University, where I worked for many years, should be presented with a copy of *What ELSE Your Boss Never Told*

*You* along with their diploma. *What ELSE Your Boss Never Told You* is not a simple check-list or one-size-fits-all book. Rather, the author recognizes the uniqueness of each leader/manager and the nature of their mission and personnel. Like all good teachers, Winters is effective because he can hold your attention by connecting the material to the reader.

Craig Virnelson<br>Kevley Technologies

*What ELSE your Boss Never Told You* is a great addition to Winters' collection of managerial books. Real-life examples of what to do and NOT to do (and those are the real things your boss *never* tells you). Winters intertwines practical ideas with interesting stories. A quick and easy read. Even someone like me, who has been managing for more than 15 years, learned a few new tricks!

Tammy Hughes, CPC, CPPM

In the same way that we aren't given a human operating manual to make sense of life, or a parenting manual at the birth of our kids, in our careers most of us are not blessed with a manager's quick start manual as we transition to a leadership role.

Gary Winters, in *What Your Boss Never Told You*, bridges this knowledge and experience gap with poignant anecdotes, razor sharp insights and actionable ways to jump start your career as well as that of your team, when leadership and management become mission critical. It includes just about everything you wanted to know but didn't know how to ask with respect to getting started in management, and includes some timeless gems for the seasoned manager as well.

I wish somebody had shared these insights with me early in my career! This will be required reading for those I have the privilege and responsibility to mentor on the road ahead.

Neville Billimoria
Senior Vice President & Chief Advocacy Officer
Mission Federal Credit Union

Gary Winters is the Yoda of management consultants! Reading *What Your Boss Never Told You* is like having a wise, experienced, and articulate guide by your side – offering you powerful, practical advice.

Keep this little book within easy reach – so you can refer to it on a regular basis. The practices and principles he writes about will make you a better leader.

Eric Klein<br>
Principal, Dharma Consulting

*What ELSE Your Boss Never Told You is a* solid piece of work. The stories on the X Factor have a lot of punch. The chapter that focuses on the importance of being effective, not being "nicer" is worth the purchase just for itself. The piece on loyalty is spot on. This book is a terrific follow-up to *What Your Boss Never Told You* – but stands on its own quite well. Do yourself a favor – if you haven't read the first book, get them both. For what you'd pay for a couple of cups of coffee, you won't regret it.

Robin Reid<br>
Organization Consultant (Retired)

While reading *What Your Boss Never Told You*, I saw myself on nearly every page. I was either nodding my head in agreement or letting out a low hum as I thought, "I wish I had thought of that when I had to supervise people." This book will undoubtedly help new supervisors and managers who, as is so rightly pointed out, are never told the full length, width, and depth of their new positions.

Let me add this is a book all managers and supervisors should read, whether they are new on the job or not.

I believe that a person should leave at least three things as a legacy. One is a box of personal journals, the second is a gallery of photographs, and the third is a library of books. I want *What Your Boss Never Told*

*You* to be part of my library when my descendants review the things that have had an influence on me.

David Royall
Retired Air Traffic Control Manager


What a wonderful tool for any new manager, or any manager humble enough to admit that they might be rusty in a few areas! *What Your Boss Never Told You* is a quick and often humorous read that offers foundational tips and how-to's to succeed as a manager at any level.

June Dudas
Assistant Director

*What Your Boss Never Told You* is an excellent, concise book for new and not-so-new managers. I enjoyed reading the principles about "flowing up," "flowing down," and letting the team figure out how to do the work. There is a key section on moral values and leadership – good to see someone emphasize that openly.

The most important section of the book for me was the chapter on consensus. It improves my leadership skills by understanding better what consensus really involves. I recommend Gary's book to those who appreciate acquiring new knowledge from a pro.

Donald W. Larson<br>San Marcos, CA

I herd "cats and turtles" for a living. That is to say, I manage others: employees, contractors, and clients. Learning to do so effectively doesn't come quickly – it takes experience, and much of that experience is often gained the hard way. *What ELSE Your Boss*

*Never Told You* is a refreshing breath of truth about the real world – what works, what doesn't, and why – for all the different types of people I manage. If you learn best, like I do, from stories, you'll love this book. The conversational style and the abundance of real-life anecdotes make this a keeper.

Timothy Lee<br>
Construction Project Manager

# What ELSE Your Boss Never Told You

Copyright © 2018 by Gary Winters

All rights reserved.

No part of this book may be reproduced in any form or by any electronic or mechanical means, including information storage and retrieval systems, without written permission from the author, except for the use of brief quotations in a book review.

## Dedication

For Kelly – You're my number one fan, as I am yours.

## Table of Contents

What Readers Are Saying ........................................ ii
Dedication .......................................................... xiii
Acknowledgments .............................................. xvi
Foreword ............................................................. xx
Introduction .......................................................... 1
**Section One: Straight Talk ............................... 11**
Chapter 1: Follower Fatigue ................................ 13
Chapter 2: Motivation 101 .................................. 28
Chapter 3: The X-Factor ...................................... 38
Chapter 4: Do Nice Managers Ever Finish First? 53
Chapter 5: What Makes People Loyal ................. 69
**Section Two: Leadership ................................. 79**
Chapter 6: Doing the Right Thing ....................... 81
Chapter 7: When I Want Your Opinion .............. 93
Chapter 8: Program Your RAS for Success ...... 102
Chapter 9: Three Words Leaders Hesitate to Say
............................................................................ 114
Chapter 10: Give 'em the Kool-Aid .................. 124
Chapter 11: The More Things Change .............. 135
**Section Three: Communication ..................... 152**
Chapter 12: How Effective Leaders Talk .......... 154

Chapter 13: How Ineffective Leaders Talk ....... 173
Chapter 14: Get Off Your But ........................... 190
Chapter 15: Sixteen Seconds of Silence ............ 197
Chapter 16: Seriously – There Are Four Kinds of Truth? .............................................................. 205
**Section Four: Offbeat and Unusual ............... 209**
Chapter 17: What Do Fireflies Have to Do with It? ........................................................................ 210
Chapter 18: Team Building with Tee Shirts ...... 218
Afterword ......................................................... 223
About the author .............................................. 227

# Acknowledgments

*"How do you thank someone who has taken you from crayons to perfume? It isn't easy, but I'll try,"*

So sings Lulu in "To Sir With Love." How can I possibly thank all the people who've helped shape this book?

It won't be easy, but I'll try.

Countless folks have impacted my career in leadership development:

The people I managed over the years, who lived through both my mistakes and achievements, helping shape my leadership style

The people I've worked for, who provided me an almost endless source of good (and not so good) examples of leadership in action

The people I've had the opportunity to coach on their leadership aptitude

The thousands of people who've attended my leadership workshops, who shared their own stories and held me accountable for the practicality and usefulness of the things we discussed

All of these people helped me understand what works, and what doesn't. They are my real-world opportunity to "field-test" every tip, technique, approach, and model that is presented in my books.

*What ELSE Your Boss Never Told You* was influenced directly by some talented people I want to thank by name. Their contributions were enormously helpful and for their help I am quite grateful.

**Kelly Burr** is my unofficial "Gentle Reader in Chief." She endured countless chapter draft readings, giving me the benefit of a neutral perspective. Not once did she express any impatience as I asked her repeatedly if I could read a few pages to her and solicit her input. She was invaluable.

**Jan Arzooman** is my editor, and she's simply amazing. There's none better. She challenged unclear passages with tact, offered many apt suggestions on style, and cleaned up the grammar flawlessly. It takes a knack for editing someone's work who likes to write in a conversational style, and Jan does it well.

Several people volunteered to be "beta" readers, charged with the task of reading an early draft and giving me suggestions and advice. Thanks must be given for the thoughtful input and insight received from **Tammy Hughes**, **Dr. Trudy Sopp**, **Craig Bronson**, **Tim** Lee, **Betsy Virnelson** and others who wanted to remain anonymous.

Finally, I want to thank *everyone* who has contributed to my growth as a person and as a professional. Whether you encouraged me and help me stretch or knocked me upside the head because I needed a reality pill, whether you embraced my creativity or reminded me of the reality I was facing in the moment, whether you applauded me or gave me a dose of straight talk when my head was swelling inappropriately, I am grateful.

# Foreword

Let me start by saying there are very few people for whom I would agree to write a foreword. If I'm going to do this, I need know the author's work to be willing to put my name behind what he or she has to say. I have read all six books Gary Winters has written – and each of them is bursting with practical tips that are demonstrably "tried and true." When I learned he was writing a sequel to What Your Boss Never Told You and he asked me to consider penning a foreword, I was 100% confident it would be a genuinely helpful book before I'd read a single word. When he sent me the draft, my belief was sustained.

As someone who's worked in learning and organization development for over 20 years, I've read countless management books promising tons of advice. Sadly, far too often they're filled with jargon, hard-to-apply models, and consultant-speak. They often leave you trying to figure out how you're supposed to apply the content. I think you'd agree your time is too precious to spend with a book without tips you can use right away. I'm happy to report you won't find that here.

That's just not Gary's approach. He has learned over the years what really works; he's applied what he's learned first-hand as both as a manager and as a coach and facilitator. Once again, he's captured a fresh batch of ideas in a new, easy-to-read, eminently practical book. Within these pages are concepts and techniques that have been "field-tested" and passed the tests of practicality and usefulness.

$$\Omega \quad \Omega \quad \Omega$$

I've known Gary for well over a decade. I've read his books and had the pleasure of seeing him in action. A few years ago, after he published What Your Boss Never Told You – A Quick-Start Guide for New Managers, he approached me in my role as Executive Director of the Centre for Organizational Effectiveness with a wonderful idea. What if he were to turn some of the concepts in this book into a two-day training program for new leaders? By the end of the conversation, S.T.A.R.T. (Supervisor Transition and Readiness Training) was born. In partnership with the Centre, Gary has facilitated this popular program over 45 times since then to over 1,000 participants who've had the unique opportunity to experience his wisdom "live" and pick his brain.

When we first launched S.T.A.R.T. our goal was to provide new supervisors with a kick-start on their leadership journey by exploring four topics:

- What Are You Getting Yourself Into?
- Understanding Change and Transition,
- Practical Situations You're Likely to Face, and
- How to Create a Transition Action Plan

What we *didn't* anticipate was attracting participants who had been in their positions for a while – and how they would find huge value in the program, often commenting "I've learned a lot. I wish I'd known this stuff before!"

Even more surprising to us was the number of people who attended not yet knowing whether they should follow a career path in supervision. These are people who are curious, but not yet convinced they should position themselves, or accept the nudge from their boss, to become a supervisor. We've found participants like these often reach one of two conclusions as a result of their S.T.A.R.T. experience:

- "I've fallen in love with the idea of becoming a supervisor and all that entails!" or
- "It's clearly not for me!"

You can imagine the benefits of these insights for both the participants and their organizations. False career steps are no fun for anyone and nor cost-effective for any organization. But, until you've explored what it's *really like* to be one, it's hard to know whether supervision is the job for you. S.T.A.R.T. helps people make an informed decision and, should they choose to become a supervisor, the tools and techniques to land well in your new position.

Gary is an incredible storyteller who is able to present the realities of supervision – and the keys to succeed. That's what sets him apart and probably explains the waiting list for the workshop. Most of us learn best through stories and anecdotes, real-life examples and illustrations. Gary has mastered this craft in person and on the printed page.

In S.T.A.R.T. workshops, I've watched participants asking questions like:

- "What other wisdom do you have for me?"
- "How would you handle my particular situation?
- "I see how what you just shared would work for this situation, but what about *that* one?"

In his answers, Gary shows his knack for simplifying what often seems complex. He's able to take complicated issues, like bringing out the best in your staff, or correcting a performance shortfall, or communicating your vision and values, and reducing them to bite-sized nuggets you can apply immediately.

Now, if you can't attend a S.T.A.R.T. workshop, I've got good news: there's an alternative – these two books: *What Your Boss Never Told You* and *What ELSE Your Boss Never Told You*. Questions that have been raised over the years since S.T.A.R.T. was launched, together with new scenarios that emerged during all those workshops created the energy for the book you're about to explore. These are the additional tips and techniques that Gary couldn't fit into his first book, What Your Boss Never Told You, or represent ideas which hadn't yet been born. You're about to benefit from decades of Gary's experience managing and coaching leaders at all levels, as well as the 1,000+ participants who have asked him for the kind of practical advice you're looking for as well.

Whether you're a new leader, a leader with a bit of experience, or someone who's wondering where you should aspire to supervision, you'll find what you need to know in these two volumes.

Let me share one more thought: the beautiful thing about the What Your Boss pair of books is that you can pick one up, open to page 5 and start reading and get as much value as starting on page 55. There are gems throughout and even if you only have ten minutes to take a quick look, you'll be rewarded with an immediate insight you can apply. *What ELSE Your Boss Never Told You*, along with its predecessor, becomes something you will reference for years to come.

Best of luck on your leadership journey,

Sommer Kehrli,
Executive Director
The Centre for Organization Effectiveness

## Introduction

Congratulations!

You're about to become, or recently became, the person in charge. The new boss. The new manager, the new supervisor. You are at the beginning, or perhaps in the midst of, a unique and exciting transition from being what's often called an *individual contributor* to becoming a person who directs the work of others.

You might be excited and eager to begin, but you might also be wondering – what are you getting yourself into? Are you ready for this? Do you know how to hit the ground running?

Too many people are promoted into a leadership role with a hearty handshake, an affirmation of support – "You'll be *great* at this position!" – and a start date: "You start on Monday. Good luck." And that's it.

What's missing is an orientation to the challenges, pitfalls, rewards, and reality of their new job. That's where *What ELSE Your Boss Never Told You – More Timely Tips for New Managers* comes in. It's a follow-up to an earlier book, *What Your Boss Never Told You – A Quick-Start Guide for New Managers*, with completely new material that just didn't fit the first time around.

Last year, I bought a new car. It came with some materials in the glove compartment including a maintenance schedule, a 456-page Owner's Manual, a 282-page Starlink Multimedia Navigation owner's manual, and a 27-page Quick Reference Guide. All together, they are housed in a 2" thick portfolio.

Bear in mind, this isn't a fancy car – it's a Subaru Forester.

Before I drove off the lot, the salesman gave me a quick overview of the features and controls in the car. Then he handed me the keys and said, "You're going to *love* this car. Good luck!"

Over the next few days, I reviewed the Quick Reference Guide. I learned a lot of practical information. I programmed the radio and set the correct time. I learned how to set the screen to view what I wanted to see, such as fuel consumption, miles-per-gallon, and so on. Now, with nearly 12,000 miles on it, I'm quite comfortable operating the car. On the other hand, I've *never* read the Owner's Manual – but I've kept it just in case.

These two books – *What Your Boss Never Told You* and *What ELSE Your Boss Never Told You* are the equivalent of Quick Reference Guides for your new management position, with the advantage that they're written in a casual, almost conversational tone with few ten-dollar words. It's almost as though we're sitting in a café having a conversation. The chapters are brief and to the point.

You can read either one first and then the other. You can even read the chapters in either book in any order. Most likely, you could read either book in one setting (perhaps on an airplane going to a conference) – but I don't recommend that. You will retain more, and put more into practice, if you read a chapter a day, or a week, and give some thought as to how you could incorporate its ideas into your management practice. Consider taking notes or keeping a journal. Research has shown when you write things down, you're more able to access important ideas later.

## Why two books?

About eight years ago, I published *What Your Boss Never Told You* and then created a two-day workshop called S.T.A.R.T. (Supervisors Transition and Readiness Training). It was unexpected and delightful to see *Boss* became my best-selling (of five) books. Since that time, thousands of people have attended the workshop, read the book, or both.

When *Boss* was written, it included five sections each with a few chapters:

- Your transition
- Your new role
- Your new team
- Your new work, and
- Three more things that didn't fit elsewhere

Since its publication, and after facilitating countless S.T.A.R.T. programs, it became clear that there was more to offer than the first book's 120 pages. But that's a dilemma that's easily solved – write another! *What ELSE* is new material not found in the original *Boss*. It has four sections:

- Straight talk
- Leadership
- Communication
- Two more things that didn't fit elsewhere

These books are a collection of ideas about how to *think* about the new job, not tutorials on (for example) how to delegate, how to manage your time, or how to conduct a corrective interview. I leave that to others. In the first book, you'll explore (among other things):

- Why you should keep your dial set to WIIFM

- The three kinds of employees you'll be managing
- How to bury a dead horse
- How managing people is like operating a floor sander
- What part of 2+2=4 belongs to you

In *What ELSE*, you'll find chapters on (among other things):

- Finding your X-Factor
- Why nice people can be terrible managers (and vice versa)
- How to get someone to talk who doesn't want to
- How to use fireflies to improve your management practice
- What to do about follower fatigue

## By the way, I'm not knocking your boss!

Occasionally, I'm asked if I believe your boss is *deliberately* keeping you uninformed about the "inside skinny" about your new role, based on the titles of these books. Not at all. Simply put, my experience is that most managers aren't as skilled – or committed – to developing new managers as we might like them to be. Most weren't coached themselves when they took their first management position, so they have no memory of how such a process could be helpful. Plus, they have many priorities at any given time, and getting you ready is just one of them. They're not ignoring these conversations because they believe these are secrets you must unlock for yourself; more likely they simply haven't put that much thought into it.

Calling the first book *What Your Boss Never Told You* was (in my opinion) a clever way to get it into more hands. After all, *How to Be a Better Manager* just isn't that sexy a title. It probably won't sell – and if it doesn't, people like you won't get the benefit from what's between its covers. After that, *What ELSE* is a natural title for the sequel.

I'm *not* knocking your boss. I'm piggy-backing on whatever you've been told about the road ahead to help you land more smoothly in your new position. These books help fill the gap between *what you already know* and *what you need to know* to become a competent manager. They pick up where many managers who've promoted someone to a management role often leave off.

## A bit about me.

As a leadership coach, workshop facilitator, and author of six books, I've had the privilege of working with leaders in over 300 large and small organizations, in the public and private sector. You might enjoy my blog, *The Leadership Almanac*, [www.garywinters.com](www.garywinters.com), which has a straightforward and powerful mission: to *simplify* what successful leaders do so others can do these things as well. Thousands of people visit the site every year to get valuable insights – for free. There you can also see my services and client portfolio.

My passion has always been to find out how effective leaders "tick" and then teach what I've learned to others.

Ready? Let's get started (again)…

## Section One: Straight Talk

We begin with some straight talk – plain, honest speech about a number of things everyone should be thinking about as they take charge of a group of people. Things often overlooked when folks are promoted, which can have an enormous impact on their success. Things I wish someone had discussed with *me* before I took charge.

- Leadership gurus say we're in the midst of a "leadership crisis" that has led to "follower fatigue" – how will that impact your new position"
- The simple question, "How do I motivate my people?" has led to over 100,000 books about motivation on amazon.com. What do you really need to know?

- What's your X-Factor?
- Do "nice" managers finish last?
- What makes people loyal to their leader?

# Chapter 1: Follower Fatigue

Stepping into a new leadership position is challenging for everyone. You have to find your bearings. You may have to put out fires before you feel confident being in charge. From time to time, you might find yourself waxing nostalgic for the "good old days" when you were an individual contributor, responsible only for yourself. In addition, there's something you may not have considered at all.

Your new staff will be looking at you through what might be called a dirty lens. That is to say, they're looking at you, but they might be seeing someone else. Maybe it's their old boss. Maybe it's *any* boss – or all previous supervisors rolled into one. Maybe it's their ideal supervisor. They're projecting on you what they've seen before – or what they hope to see. It's not conscious; it just is.

Given that, one of your first challenges will be to clean their glasses. Clarify their vision, if you will. Establish yourself – the real you – as the new person in charge. That's not new – every new leader has had to do it. But nowadays, there's an additional twist on this process you might want to consider. There are many who feel we're all living in a worldwide *leadership crisis* – and it could have an enormous influence on your transition.

## What's happened to leadership?

Pundits, leadership gurus, academics and others are engaged in a spirited dialogue about the state of leadership on the world stage today. This debate is important to consider, because it has implications for *every* leader – whether you're perched on a global platform or sitting in a cramped conference room with your department. In other words, it has implications for *you*.

Alon Ben-Meir, Senior Fellow and expert on global leadership at NYU, frames the conversation like this: "We have yet to find any leader – and I challenge anyone to name one – who can rise to meet the awesome challenges we face today. Undeniably, we are witnessing a *dearth of leadership* reflecting our state of affairs and conditions nearly everywhere."

Frank Giustra, Canadian businessman and filmmaker, weighs in: "Where is Winston Churchill when you need him? Someone who has not only the courage to make the right decisions but who could inspire others to follow in times of crisis?"

The non-profit World Economic Forum surveyed 1,200 economists and other experts in 2015 and found that *85% of them* believe we are suffering a global leadership crisis.

Where is this angst coming from?

Recollect how the great issues of the last decade have played out. The United States (and much of the world) has been awash with complicated troubles, such as (in no particular order):

- The Great Recession
- Collapsing housing markets
- Wondering whether huge international organizations are "too big to fail"
- Unemployment figures that approached 10% in 2010
- Terrorism
- Environmental disasters from the Deepwater Oil Spill in the Gulf of Mexico to hurricanes in Houston, Florida, and Puerto Rico to wildfires, floods, and drought

- The polarization of politics
- The #MeToo movement, exposing dozens of entertainers, politicians, business leaders, and others to charges of sexual misconduct

Granted, some of these situations have improved. In America, we're no longer wallowing in a recession; the housing market has stabilized; unemployment has dropped to about 4%. But too many solutions stubbornly remain unclear. The longer these problems appear intractable, the more they lead to an *erosion of faith* in leaders who don't seem able to deliver.

## A sustained leadership crisis creates follower fatigue

When people don't see solutions to problems emerging, when people lose hope these questions will ever be solved, eventually they become:

- Apathetic
- Angry
- Bitter
- Cynical
- Numb
- Resigned, or
- A combination of the above

That's *follower fatigue*, the state of being exhausted with what people perceive as ineffective leadership. The evidence that people are "turning off" to leadership is overwhelming. Surveys and polls consistently show that the public reports little trust or confidence in:

- **Government**: A Pew Research Center survey in 2017 reported that only 20% of Americans surveyed trusted their government would "do the right thing."

- **Business**: The Edelman Trust Barometer periodically surveys tens of thousands of people in dozens of countries; in 2016 they reported that 63% of respondents said that CEOs were "not at all" or "only somewhat" credible.
- **Banks**: Gallop found in 2017 that just 32% of Americans expressed "a great deal" or "quite a lot" of confidence in banks.
- **Media**: A Reuters/Ipsos poll revealed that just 39% of Americans expressed a "great deal" or "some" confidence in the press.
- **Public figures**: As more and more entertainers, athletes, politicians, and others fall from

grace, people are no longer reacting with shock, but with weariness.

- **The boss**: There are no stats to cite, but it stands to reason if people are unhappy or disillusioned with other authority figures, this transfers to their boss as well.

If they're suffering from follower fatigue, the people on your team no longer fully or easily believe, endorse, or support the messages from their organization's leaders any more, whether they come from the head of your enterprise, or your director, or your manager, or *even you*. Instead they increasingly interpret these messages as business-speak, hype, rationalization, hoopla, or phony "kumbaya."

When they hear things like:

- "We'll keep layoffs to a minimum."
- "We'll never sell the organization."
- "Your retirement program is safe."
- "It's highly unlikely we'll relocate."
- "People are our most important resource."

They see their colleagues:
- Lose their pensions or retirement benefits
- Lose their jobs through layoffs or mergers
- Lose their jobs to younger, cheaper "talent"

Employees listen to their leaders talk about their vision, mission, and values, and react with skepticism if not cynicism. They've got follower fatigue. *Can you blame them?*

## What can you do?

Here's a surprising suggestion. Don't worry about the leadership crisis; *acknowledge it*. Let it unwind, evolve, or get better or worse without your active concern. After all, you're not going to solve the question of peace in the Middle East, right?

Instead, put your focus on something you *can* do something about: follower fatigue – in particular, on how that is playing out with your new team. That's where you can make a difference; it's where you can have an impact. Make it your intention to be the leader your staff wants and deserves. Be aware that you're stepping into your new position with all the baggage that's attached to leaders these days and do what can be done in your sphere of influence. Think global but act local.

People – even if they're jaded or suspicious of leadership in general – will eventually respond to truth, honesty, transparency, and straight talk. They may be doubtful at first. After all, you're the new boss, and they're likely to be skeptical. They've had many bosses before you. But underneath all their uncertainty, there are hearts and minds yearning for a leader they can trust.

Whatever your other priorities when you assume your new position, perhaps your most important will be to earn their trust. Don't fret if it doesn't come quickly. It will take a while. People are invested in their fatigue, after all. But trust will come, if you're willing to do a number of things consistently over that period of time. Five of the most important:

- **Be honest.** Tell people the truth as best you can. Yes, there may be things you *can't* tell them in a particular situation (perhaps the information is confidential, for example). In that case, tell them what you *can* tell them truthfully.
- **Be authentic.** Be real; be genuine. Don't project an image. Be who you are – warts and all.
- **Be compassionate.** Take a stand for what's right. Do what's right, even when no one's watching.
- **Be humble.** Entrepreneur Tim Fargo, a bestselling leadership author and speaker who founded

the second biggest insurance fraud company in the United States, puts it this way: "Remember, leadership is service, not position." Put *their* needs ahead of *your* needs. Be quick to give them credit and be just as quick to take the blame when things go awry.

- **Be available.** Be approachable. Be visible. Be there when the stuff hits the fan.

Ω   Ω   Ω

A Chinese fable tells the story of a farmer who had an enigmatic way of responding to situations as they unfolded. One day his old, frail horse ran away. A neighbor commiserated with him, saying, "That's bad news!"

The farmer replied, "Good news, bad news, who can say?"

A few days later the horse returned, along with three wild horses. The neighbor was struck by the farmer's good fortune, saying, "That's great news!"

The farmer replied, "Good news, bad news, who can say?"

Later that day, the farmer's son took one of the wild horses for a romp in the pasture. The horse threw him, breaking his legs. "That's terrible!" said the neighbor.

"Good news, bad news, who can say?"

Later that week, soldiers came to the village to conscript all able-bodied men for a campaign in the north. But they rejected the farmer's son.

---

*Good news, right? Who's to say?*

---

According to experts, you're stepping into a leadership role at a time when there's a worldwide leadership crisis, which in turn has led to a pandemic of follower fatigue.

Good news, bad news – who can say?

Decide for yourself. Be discouraged, or see it as a wonderful opportunity. Just don't ignore it. Winston Churchill put it well:

---

*"A pessimist sees the difficulty in every opportunity. An optimist sees the opportunity in every difficulty."*

---

Be an optimist.

## Chapter 2: Motivation 101

It's by far the most popular question at the beginning of my S.T.A.R.T. workshop – *How do I motivate my people?"*

The question is asked in many ways:

- "How do I light a fire under Joanne? She seems completely burned out."
- "Like every job, my staff has to do some things no one really wants to do. How do I get them to be a little more willing to do the unpopular tasks?"
- "My team is in a slump. We've just finished a very busy season, and everyone is off their game. How do I turn that around?"

- "Zach is slacking off lately. Tardy, too many personal phone calls, inattention to detail. How can I get him motivated and back on track?"

Usually, it's a simple question: "How do I get people to do what they're supposed to do?" but occasionally it's all dressed up: "How can I foster enthusiasm, energy, and commitment?" Let's take a closer look.

In my workshops, we occasionally do a two-round exercise to start the discussion on motivation. It works like this: In Round One, a volunteer is sent outside the room while those remaining choose an object (such as a water carafe, or a flip chart marker) that the volunteer has to find when they return. The volunteer is summoned, and another volunteer plays his "supervisor" during the hunt.

The "supervisor" is given a rolled-up newspaper and an instruction. As soon as the original volunteer begins navigating the room, the "supervisor" is to give him or her feedback in the form of a (light) whack on the shoulders whenever the volunteer moves in the wrong direction, that is, away from the hidden object. If the volunteer moves in the right direction, the supervisor does nothing.

*In other words, the volunteer soon learns that no news is good news.*

Round One doesn't last long. Often, after three or four rolled-up newspaper corrections, the volunteer gives up.

Round Two begins with a fresh volunteer and a new chosen object. This time, there is no "supervisor." Instead, all of the participants are asked to do a drum roll on their tables when the volunteer begins to move. Specifically, each time the volunteer moves closer to the object, the drum roll grows louder. If they move away from the object, the drum roll stops. As they get closer, the drum roll gets louder until the object is found.

In other words, the group keeps "catching 'em doing something right."

The object is often found quite quickly. No one has ever quit as a volunteer in Round Two.

Motivation is a popular subject for managers, if the 100,000+ books you can find on amazon.com is any measure. If you want to explore it more deeply, you might look for resources on these five theories of motivation:

- Herzberg's Two-Factor Theory
- Maslow's Hierarchy of Needs
- The Hawthorne Effect
- Expectancy Theory
- Weiner's Three-Dimensional Theory of Attribution

They all have fascinating implications for leaders, and are well worth learning. But for now, let's simplify the subject and consider some practical ideas you can put to use right away.

## 1. Train yourself to notice, and comment, on what's going well

We're all creatures of habit. Too many managers have a habit of noticing what's going wrong – and moving to fix it. They spend little time catching people doing something right, let alone saying something when they do.

"It's not my job to pat them on the head all the time," a coaching client once complained. "They're here to do a job; they're grownups; they don't need me to babysit them."

That mindset is pervasive, and it's counter-productive. You *are* here to notice – and acknowledge – good performance. That *is* your job. Why? Because the research is clear:

---

*What gets rewarded gets repeated.*

---

A pat on the back, a simple "Thank you!" or a Post It note left on their desk goes a long way to get an employee to repeat whatever they've done. "I love how you handled that disgruntled customer," will do far more to increase the number of times customers are handled with grace than the comment "Don't *ever* talk to a customer that way again!" will.

## 2. Don't be the "no news is good news" kind of manager.

We've all worked for one. "I haven't heard anything from the boss, so I must be doing something right." Maybe it's human nature to notice only the bad news. Look at today's headlines: bad news. What are they saying on CNN? Bad news. What's in the newspaper? Bad news. We become so accustomed to filter *in* the things that are wrong we rarely notice what's going right.

Here's something you can do: Train yourself to reverse that habit. The next time you go out for dinner, practice *noticing* everything that's going right about the experience. Did you get seated promptly? Did your server greet you promptly? Did someone bring you water and take a drink order efficiently? Was the food appealing as it appeared on the plate? Did it taste good? If there was a problem with any of the food, did they take care of it quickly?

Maybe your answers are a combination of yes and no. Either way, here's part two: After you *notice* the things that went right, *say something* about it to the appropriate person. That's it! Unless something went terribly wrong, pay *no* attention to those things. Just notice and comment on what went right.

Thank the host, or the server. Compliment the chef (even if through the server). Smile at the person who brings you a beverage. Practice noticing what went right and acknowledging the person who did it well. As it becomes second nature, transfer the habit to managing your team. You'll never again be accused of being the "no news is good news" kind of manager. Notice and acknowledge. Over and over.

## 3. Motivation isn't what you do *to* people. It's what you do *for* them.

Motivation isn't just a collection of techniques. It's not magic dust you sprinkle over your staff. It's not a four-step process, and there is no standard script. Learning to motivate is not like learning to delegate or manage your time or conduct an interview. It's not about what you do as much as it's about who you are.

Some managers have come to believe that motivation can be boiled down to two things – the carrot and the stick. Reward people for doing things right and punish them for doing it wrong.

Motivation is the conscious process of unleashing the potential of others. We are all *intrinsically* motivated by lots of things:

wanting to make a contribution, wanting to do good work, wanting to be valued, etc.

Effective leaders are those who bring out our best. They appeal to our natural desire to matter – to make a difference – to make the world a little bit better. People respond to acknowledgement, being selected for better projects, the chance to learn something new.

Create an environment where your staff feels acknowledged and valued and believes there's a genuine opportunity to grow, and you'll soon have a motivated staff. Make the environment caustic, the work boring and meaningless, and interpersonal relationships melodramatic, and you'll find yourself asking, "How do I motivate my people?"

## Chapter 3: The X-Factor

For decades, people have debated whether leadership aptitude is something you're born with, or something you learn. Perhaps, as I believe, it's a combination of both.

You can learn how to:

- Conduct great interviews and make good hiring decisions
- Lead successful change efforts
- Conduct effective meetings
- Coach someone who's going through a difficult time
- Write a useful performance review

But there are some things that simply can't be learned or taught. One is your X-Factor. This is a trait or disposition you bring to the table that is uniquely yours. You've probably used this talent throughout your life (perhaps without realizing it was what made you unique).

## It's all about finding calm in the chaos

A friend of mine has worked for years as the right-hand assistant to a catering chef. It's a high-stress, sometimes frantic environment, calling for attention to detail, technical expertise, and the intestinal fortitude to work under pressure. If you've ever seen Chef Gordon Ramsey in action, you know how quickly the restaurant environment can become a very unpleasant experience.

Kelly, however, has an X-Factor. She has a knack for juggling all the balls in the air while remaining calm. The more others get frazzled, the more Kelly becomes composed.

To watch her directing traffic is like watching a conductor leading an orchestra. She gets everyone to do what needs to be done in a way that seems effortless to others – who don't realize the thousand details she's processing throughout the event.

Kelly has the ability to remain calm in the midst of chaos. When others see a thousand details demanding attention, she can triage in an instant and focus on what's most important. Her ability to do this is natural and part of her essence.

This doesn't just show up when she's catering. I've seen her deal with family health emergencies the same way. Others are becoming frantic, not sure what to do. Kelly gets into her zone and brings order to the pandemonium. Of course, training may have honed her professional skill, but based on the stories she tells of her childhood, she's been doing this all her life. Remaining calm in a storm is Kelly's X-Factor.

## "I almost thought you were invisible."

One of my mentors and colleagues was Larry, who may have been the best workshop facilitator I ever knew. It was his job to conduct retreats, team-building workshops, strategic planning sessions – that sort of thing. He would remind people the word "facilitate" means "to make things easier." It was his job to make the task at hand easier for those involved. He'd help create the ground rules, ask the right questions, record group decisions on flip charts, encourage everyone to make themselves heard, and so on.

He was invariably focused on the *process* unfolding in the meeting, and let the *content* belong to others. His concern was the "how," not the "what." He didn't own the meeting – that was something that belonged to others. He never voiced an opinion about what a final decision should be, but instead offered methods that would help the group make an agreement they could support. A humble man, it was a point of pride for Larry to be complimented by someone who would say, "I can't believe how much we accomplished – and how little I noticed you were even in the room."

His goal was to help the group get the job done without having to be the star or even a highly visible consultant. People would tell him, "Clearly you did some magic in there – but I'll be darned if I can put my finger on exactly what you did!"

Larry's X-Factor was his ability to be at the center of a group meeting without having to be the center of attention. He wasn't sought after because he was clever, or witty, or flashy. Rarely can people even recall what he wore to the event, or a story he may have told. But he got results.

## When you spoke with Jim, you felt important

Jim's a well-respected figure in his market-dominating organization. He's a visionary, he's a compelling communicator, he's tireless, and he's legendary in his knowledge of his organization's products and services.

He also has the knack of being able to make anyone think that they are the most important person in the world to him at a given moment. He demonstrates it daily with people at all levels of his organization, from the shop floor to the executive suite.

No one has concluded a conversation with Jim without believing he thinks they're valuable, their contribution is significant, and they've been heard. Few things bring out the best in people more than believing their boss (or teacher, mentor, partner, friend, or whoever is important to them) thinks they're important.

I doubt Jim was taught how to do that. He brought that quality to his leadership practice from deep within his personality. He's been doing it all his life. Perhaps you'd argue that Jim is simply a good listener, and that's a skill anyone can learn (or improve). I disagree.

Just saying Jim is a good listener is like saying Dr. Phil (McGraw) is a good television host, or Winston Churchill was a good politician, or Meryl Streep is a good actor. Those statements are true, but they fail to acknowledge that these people had X-Factors that set them apart from others who otherwise did very similar things. Dr. Phil's X-Factor is his sophisticated country charm. ("How's that working for you?") Churchill's was his tenacity coupled with optimism. Streep's is her monomaniacal attention to detail.

## Fire, Ready, Aim!

Then there's Tom. A former highway patrol officer, he moved into a management role in a large manufacturing organization and soon excelled at his ability to drive his department to extraordinary levels of achievement.

To some, he was an SOB to work for, rough around the edges and not the sort of person who would be described as "politically correct." Most would admit privately, on the other hand, that once you'd worked for him, your own performance quickly rose to another level. Why? When you worked for Tom, things got done.

He was rash, impulsive, and quick to make decisions. Fortunately, most of the time he made damn good ones. Training and coaching helped him improve *how* he made them (for instance, learning when to include or exclude his staff and others in the process), but no training could make him more decisive.

Tom was predisposed to act.

Those who worked for Tom, people who struggled with the molasses that permeates bureaucratic decision-making in many large organizations, found in him a champion for their initiatives.

For Tom, his X-Factor was decisiveness.

## Problems? What problems?

Sally is tone-deaf to negativity. Simply doesn't hear it – or if she does, she refuses to acknowledge it. To work for Sally is to learn to rephrase "I've got a problem" into "I've got an opportunity."

When people first meet Sally, they think it's got to be a gimmick. A technique she picked up somewhere along the line. But they soon change their minds – negativity just doesn't resonate with Sally. It's not a part of who she is – it's not in her DNA.

Sally is infectious and engaging (to the point where new staff members sometimes find it maddening). She's crazy about it. The result? People who work for Sally long enough soon find themselves trading a plate full of problems to be solved into a buffet of fascinating challenges to embrace. Challenges are *always* more compelling than difficulties.

Positivity is Sally's X-Factor.

## Almost anyone can learn to be a better leader

American organizations certainly believe so. U.S. organizations spent an estimated $15.5 billion on leadership development initiatives in 2013 (latest figures available), according to research by Deloitte, an HR consulting company. There must be a fundamental belief in the value of leadership education.

There's no doubt you'll be far more effective in your leadership practice if you study what effective leaders do. You can come to master skills that are time-tested and proven to be effective. You'll have a greater capacity to deal with what comes your way.

But you'll be even more effective if you can identify your X-Factor and leverage it as much as possible.

## What is your X-Factor?

It's probably obvious, but for many it could be hiding in plain view. Start by asking yourself a few questions:

What's my customary response to things happening in the world around me?

- I get incredibly focused
- I see patterns helping me understand how what's happened before connects with what's happening now
- I see what's absurd about the situation
- I pay attention to how people are feeling about things
- I notice the "devil in the details"
- I am energized and itching to act

What unique contribution do I bring to the situation?

- I am helpful
- I am organized
- I am available
- I am able to see what's funny about it
- I am irreverent
- I am brash

What are two or three words that people most often use to describe me?

- Impulsive, obsessive, generous
- Driven, results-oriented
- Sensitive, caring, kind
- Funny, creative, thoughtful
- Competitive, risk-taker, impulsive
- Thrifty, methodical, wise

When my coaching client Casey thought about these questions, she was not surprised at her answers:

*1. "I take my work seriously, but myself lightly."*
*2. "I'm good at putting people at ease through humor."*
*3. "They often say I'm funny, relaxed, and confident."*

As we talked, it became obvious to Casey that her warm, infectious sense of humor is an X-Factor. As she embraces it, she can take her leadership practice to another level. For example, she happens to run a fairly efficient meeting, but she wants to do it better. It will probably be her effective use of humor that will take her meetings to the next level.

Casey is witty and can use her X-Factor to put people at ease, or lower tension in a contentious meeting. That should not imply that *you* need to learn some one-liners or improve your timing when you tell a joke. The anecdote should inspire you to determine your own X-Factor, which you can acknowledge, embrace, and leverage to become the unique, effective leader you want to be.

## Chapter 4: Do Nice Managers Ever Finish First?

Nice guys finish last, right? What about nice managers?

"I don't know the keys to success, but the keys to failure are to try to please everybody." (Unknown)

The characteristics of what people think makes a good manager today are quite different from what people thought just thirty or so years ago. Through most of the twentieth century, the boss was someone who was expected to be:

- Tough
- "My way or the highway"
- Mean, gruff, and typically unapproachable

- Task-oriented – rarely someone who would be described as a "people" person
- Uncaring (and perhaps even unsympathetic) about a subordinate's personal issues

When I began my career, those notions were (thankfully!) beginning to fade. But there were still plenty of strong, no-nonsense managers with poor people skills. If you worked for one, you knew not to question their decisions or share many details of your personal life. They were the boss, and you weren't. It was as simple as that.

Today, we still find people like that in leadership roles in our organizations. They're often called dinosaurs, but unlike their reptilian brethren, they're not quite extinct. Even if you never worked for one, chances are good you know one or more in your organization.

New ways of thinking about the roles and expectations of managers – and employees – began to emerge toward the end of the twentieth century. A new paradigm completely altered the model of effective leadership. It's important to understand where these new ideas originated.

## The birth of employee involvement

Let's begin with the pioneering work of W. Edwards Deming, who conceived and widely promoted a concept that came to be called Quality Circles. This was a method of selecting groups of "rank-and-file" employees to meet regularly to address issues occurring on the assembly line. (Manufacturing was the major organizational model at the time.) For the first time, these employees were given problem-solving training, and they were charged with giving suggestions to management on how to resolve them.

It can hardly be understated how revolutionary this idea was. Employees at the time were expected to blindly follow orders from their boss, and managers were expected to have (all) the answers to complex issues. Deming was among the first to demonstrate that the people closest to a problem (line employees) would be more likely to know how to resolve it than people higher in the food chain (managers). At the time, a quite radical idea.

In fact, Deming found such strong resistance to his concepts he had to take them to Japanese automobile manufacturers first, who were still struggling to find their way in the 1960s. It was only when these companies applied these techniques and found success competing in global markets that American companies invited him to share his ideas with them.

I shall never forget a Quality Circle presentation I was invited to observe in a facility belonging to a contractor in the defense industry. When it was complete, and managers were thanking the employees for their participation, one fellow raised his hand and asked if he could offer one more thing. He was given the go-ahead.

"I've worked here for forty years. I'm going to retire in the next year or two. I just wanted to thank you for including me in this Quality Circle. *It's the first time in my career that I've actually been asked for my opinion or advice.*"

## Along comes Tom Peters

In 1982, Tom Peters published what became a best-selling book, *In Search of Excellence*. He described a simple but highly effective management technique called "Managing by Wandering Around" (MBWA), first popularized at Hewlett-Packard. It was centered on the then-innovative idea that managers would be more effective if they occasionally left their offices to (literally) wander around the workplace, checking in with employees and seeing what was going on firsthand. If this idea seems quaint to you, it's because it's wide-spread practice now, and few employees look up quizzically when their boss is spotted outside the office.

Ask someone in the restaurant business about this. They call it "Touch every table," which is in stark contrast to the old days, when managers were told to stay in "the back of the house." Nowadays, they're expected to be out front, greeting customers and finding solutions when issues arise.

As Quality Circles and ideas like MBWA gained a foothold, a pendulum began to shift toward something called Employee Involvement, which was based on the idea that there could be huge benefits from asking employees to participate in:

- Deciding how their work is done
- Making suggestions for improvement
- Setting their own goals
- Monitoring their own performance

The notion that slowly caught fire was that involved employees would be more motivated to improve their performance. Eventually, the shift from the tough boss model to a participatory employee model took hold. Leaders became more inclusive and involved with their staff. The new understanding was that to be effective, leaders needed to be more:

- Employee-focused

- Open and transparent

- Approachable – even "challengeable" by employees who might question the wisdom of decisions, strategy, or tactics

- Adept at so-called "people skills" like communication, empathy, team-building, coaching, and conflict management

# Where does being a nice person fit in?

What does all of this have to do with nice guys (men or women) getting into management positions? Is being "nice" a factor that will contribute to your success, or is it a liability?

According to Thesaurus.com, a *Mr. Nice Guy* is "a typically pleasant, likeable person who avoids causing trouble or dissension."

People who describe their managers "nice" often elaborate by saying these are people who:

- Take few risks

- Look for ways to be congenial and well-liked

- Avoid "straight-talk"

- Often seek approval from their boss, their peers, and especially their subordinates

- Ignore or avoid conflict

- Have trouble saying no

$$\Omega \quad \Omega \quad \Omega$$

Many people have come to believe that using Employee Involvement means being a "nice guy" manager. If we now expect managers to be transparent and approachable, with good people skills, does it not follow they should be nice guys (again, or gals)?

In a word, no. Being nice can't be your X-Factor (see Chapter 3). You can't rely on being a nice guy to lead people effectively.

But we have to make a distinction. If by being nice you mean things like:

- Being *tactful*, saying, "How could you have done that differently?" instead of "You idiot! What were you thinking?"

- Being *considerate*, saying, "I know this is unexpected, but I really need you to come in this weekend if you can," rather than, "I guess you'll just have to get this done on Saturday!"

- Being *respectful*, saying, "Before I decide one way or the other, I'd really like to hear you weigh in," not, "What part of my being in charge do you not understand?"

- Being *kind*, saying, "It must be worrisome, trying to find a way to balance the demands of this project with your kid's Little League schedule," rather than, "It's just a few games you'll miss. They'll soon forget all about it!"

…you're on the right track.

But, if by being nice you mean things like:

- Not telling Frank that his project plan is woefully short of detail because you're worried he'll get angry and throw a fit
- Pretending Jackie's habit of being late for meetings isn't that important because you don't want to ruffle her feathers
- Avoiding Stan's performance review because he's not going to like hearing that some of his results didn't meet standard

…you're setting yourself up for failure.

## The hidden side of nice managers

I can no longer count how many managers I've come to know over the years, either as their coach, their workshop facilitator, their colleague, or even their subordinate. There were more than a few that most folks described as "nice guys." When I think about them, I recall:

- They were often thoughtful
- They were fun to be around
- They didn't push too hard
- For them, "good enough" often was just that – good enough

Ω    Ω    Ω

Looking back, I'm struck not by what they displayed, but with what they kept hidden. No quirks. No rough edges. Nothing irritating about them at all. They rarely stood out from others, as I recall.

As a group, they had little in common – except they were nice folks. They were absolutely some of the nicest people you'd ever meet – it would be hard to find fault with them. They were cheerful, polite, and friendly. They were usually "politically correct." They worked hard not to stick their necks out or ruffle feathers. They were good people with good intentions – *but they were not good leaders.*

In contrast, I've had the privilege of working with some quite remarkable, highly successful managers who would never have been called a nice guy (or gal). Some were inspirational; some were irreverent; one or two had a knack for telling great stories to illustrate a teachable moment. They all had remarkable achievements.

But I have no doubt they would cringe if someone described them as a "nice" person. That was never their X-Factor.

---

*"At home, I am a nice guy, but I don't want the world to know," Muhammad Ali once said. "Humble people, I've found, don't get very far."*

---

This is not a knock against nice people. Far from it! We probably don't have enough of them in this world. I'm suggesting that the best *leaders* I know are hardly "nice" people: They can be impatient, or self-absorbed, or nitpickers, or aggressive, or hard-to-please. Some are clearly obsessed, or impolite, or aloof.

As a leadership coach, I work with leaders to improve their effectiveness. But I never attempt to make them "nicer."

I happen to believe that there aren't many truly effective nice leaders. As they say, nice guys finish last, right?

# Chapter 5: What Makes People Loyal

It's likely that among the things you'll want to do as you assume your leadership responsibilities is to create a loyal staff. But what exactly does that mean? It's not black-and-white.

When S.T.A.R.T. participants are asked to write (anonymous) answers on an index card to the following sentence prompt – *If my employees were loyal, they'd* _____, their responses are quite varied:

- If my employees were loyal, they'd try to do a good job all the time
- If my employees were loyal, they wouldn't second-guess or gossip about my decisions

- If my employees were loyal, they'd be willing to go the extra mile (work overtime, come in early or stay late, do the less-desirable tasks)
- If my employees were loyal, they'd put the needs of the organization (or our team) ahead of their personal needs
- If my employees were loyal, they'd stick around for a long time – not jump at the first chance of a better job somewhere else.

In table discussions, there have been those who have said, "If my employees were loyal, they'd eagerly do what they've been told, when they've been told, and how they've been told, without hesitation or question. They'd do these things for as long as I need them to do so."

These sound like excellent qualities for a printer or a fax machine, but people aren't printers or fax machines.

## What *is* a loyal employee?

Like just about everything else, the concept of employee loyalty has changed. Organizations used to have an unspoken, unwritten social contract with employees. "Come to work for us. Give us your best work, stick around, and we'll take care of you. At the end of twenty or thirty (or forty) years, we'll reward you with a pension and a gold watch."

That worked fairly well, when the boss was the all-knowing, all-powerful figure who barked orders from on high, and employees were subservient, interchangeable "worker bees" who did as they were told. Then came Employee Involvement (see Chapter Four). As employees were beginning to be asked for their input on how their work is done, or how to improve both work processes and the work product – in general, in what way to make things better in the organization, a fresh understanding of what makes a loyal employee began to emerge. Loyalty wasn't a simple matter of doing what you're told; it became something different altogether.

Jeff Haden of Inc. Magazine (www.inc.com/jeff-haden/6-qualities-of-remarkably-loyal-employees.html) offers insight into this new paradigm. He describes what he calls remarkable loyal employees as those who:

1. Treat you like a person. Not just a boss. They realize that you have your own dreams, hopes, insecurities, and fears. You're human. They want what's best for you as much as they know you want what's best for them.
2. They're willing to tell you what you may not want to hear. Let's face it. There will be times when your ideas may not work, your point of view may be skewed, and you might be making a mistake. They'll offer tactful straight talk about these issues, knowing that while you might not want to hear it (in the moment), you're far more interested in doing what's best for the organization.

3. They don't criticize you in front of others. Although lots of folks enjoy mocking, spreading gossip, or sniping about their bosses, truly loyal employees simply don't go there. They give you the respect you deserve – the respect that they expect to receive as well.
4. They disagree in private. Loyal employees know that debate and disagreement are healthy. They share their opinions as freely as you do – and they do that in private when it makes sense to do so – out of respect for you.
5. They support your decisions in public. Once a decision has been made, particularly when they've been a "devil's advocate" about it in private, loyal employees

don't try to sabotage you – they try to make it work.

6. They let you know when it's time for them to go. Let's be honest – we all want great employees to stay as long as possible. But sometimes they need to leave. Maybe there's a better job out there, or they want to relocate, or there's a family issue that has changed their priorities. Strong, loyal employees know that their departure will disrupt productivity for a time, and they're willing to let you know as far in advance as they can, because they trust that you'll handle the transition with grace. As Haden puts it, "They've put your interests ahead of theirs a number of times – and now they

know you'll do the same for them."

## How do you foster that kind of loyalty?

Here are six suggestions:

1. Act with integrity. Keep your promises, don't avoid bad news, be accessible, own your mistakes, and be honest. Remember, people will do what you do, not what you tell them to do.
2. Insist on calling out the elephant in the room when it comes to visit. Don't pretend it isn't there. Don't wait for someone else to bring it up. Don't minimize it – but don't hyperventilate, either.

It's important, and you and your team can handle it.
3. Catch people doing something right. Especially when they play "devil's advocate" in your staff meeting. Make it okay for folks to respectfully poke at ideas, plans, and suggestions. Not to be contrary for its own sake, but to find even better ideas, plans, and suggestions.
4. Praise employees in public – and confront issues in private. Just as you would like their public support and private criticism, model what this looks like with your team.
5. Practice straight talk. Demonstrate the value of coming to the point rather than beating around the bush. Learn to tell the truth

without being (or being seen as) mean-spirited. Review Chapter Four about the differences between being tactful, considerate, respectful, or kind and avoiding, ignoring, or denying something that needs to be handled.

Be grateful for loyal employees when you have them, and be willing to wish them well when it's time for them *to leave*. Whatever will be, will be.

Ω Ω Ω

Perhaps the great philosopher Anonymous had it right when he (or she) said, "Loyalty means I am down with you whether you are right or wrong, but I will tell you when you're wrong and help you get it right."

How do you get a loyal staff like that? You demonstrate your loyalty to them.

## Section Two: Leadership

Best-selling author Warren Bennis (Business school professor at University of Southern California for 35 years and the author of 30 books on leadership) says,

*"Leadership is like beauty; it's hard to define, but you know it when you see it."*

We'll take a closer look at some important aspects of leading others:

- What to do when you face the dilemma between doing the right thing (following procedure, custom, or a directive from your own boss), and doing something else which you believe in your heart is the right thing to do

- How to get your staff to give you their honest opinion about an issue

- Applying the "law of expectations" to help your staff achieve its full potential

- The power of saying, "I don't know."

- Should you be serving Kool-Aid to your staff?

- Introducing and facilitating change in your department

# Chapter 6: Doing the Right Thing

In my first book, *What Your Boss Never Told You,* we explored how leadership guru Warren Bennis compared leaders to managers. Bennis suggested that managers are people who do things right while leaders are people who do the right thing. In this chapter, we'll be talking about the risks associated with the right thing.

Remember, you're doing things right (doing them correctly) when, for example:

- You're doing it the way it's always been done
- You're following the policy manual

- You're doing what your boss, or her boss, or his boss, has told you to do

You're doing what's right, on the other hand, when you know in your heart it's what must be done, *regardless* of precedence, policy or marching orders. Here's something my own manager shared with me: in a managerial career, you'll be faced with "moments of truth" when you have to choose between doing things properly and doing what you ~~think~~ *know* is right. How do you sort that out?

It almost always arises unexpectedly. Things have been moving along as usual. People are doing their job; tasks are getting done, when suddenly, something happens. The jelly gets sucked right out of your donut. A situation presents itself and it's not going to go away. Inaction is not an option. You have two choices: resolve it "by the book" or do it another way – the way that seems like the right thing to do.

Suppose you're the manager of Parks and Recreation for a small city. Among other things, your department runs the Little League program. One day, your program coordinator comes to you with a dilemma. A mom has come to the front counter to enroll her son for this summer's schedule, but it's more than a week after the posted deadline to register new participants. She's explained that the family was out of the country for several weeks, making it impossible for her to comply within the deadline. She'd like him enrolled nonetheless.

Doing it right would mean denying her application, based on a policy that outlines when players must sign up. Making an exception might be considered unfair to others who met the deadline; it could even imperil the reputation of the department (after all, if they'd make an exception for this child, what other policies could be bent – and for whom?).

However, the mission of the department is to provide recreational opportunities to citizens, and there is nearly always room for at least one more when it comes to Little League, swimming programs, and the like. Denying this parent means preventing a youngster all the rewards of participating in what has been a memorable and important part of growing up in your community.

Let's throw another wrinkle into the mix. The mom in question happens to be a member of City Council. Does *that* change anything? Maybe or maybe not – but it clearly scrambles your eggs that morning. If you elevate the issue to your Director, what do you think you'd be told to do? However you're directed, it's still your decision.

You're facing a fork in the road. One path is proper (customary, by-the-book), with less risk. It's the *safer* path. True, you might face some criticism for following procedure, but comes with being in charge. People in authority are frequently criticized for requiring others to adhere to policy.

The other path comes with more risk. You could be hailed as a hero if it ends well, or be the goat if it goes south. Your decision will be second-guessed by the armchair quarterbacks who aren't being held accountable for the choice. It's tough out there!

Taking risks is what separates leaders from managers. Bennis understood the distinction well: "Most organizations are over-managed and under-led." Most of us, faced with the choice, will follow precedent or policy (or a direct order from our boss) more often than we follow our instinct. Perhaps that's as it should be. Organizations coalesce around agreed policies and procedures; to do otherwise is to invite chaos into the mix.

But there will be times when you simply must forge a different path – a new path – because, in your judgment, it's the best way forward. When should you do that?

No one – not a mentor, not a coach, not even this book, can tell you which path to take when you have to choose between acting as a manager or acting as a leader. That said, there are some things to consider when you find yourself in this predicament.

## Don't be afraid of what can go wrong. Focus on what can go right.

Here's how:

1. *Listen to your inner voice.* Get yourself in a quiet space. Become calm. Let go of as much "stuff" as you can, and let your inner voice begin to speak.

2. *Ask yourself – is my inner voice revealing a path?* My colleague and occasional writing partner, Eric Klein (http://wisdomheart.com) has a wonderful, almost irreverent technique that's helpful when you feel stuck. For example, I might say to him, "Let's go to lunch!" and he might respond with "Where do you want to go?" If I say, "Gee, I don't know," he'll respond with "Well, if you *did* know, where would it be?" Astonishingly, I almost always have an

answer to that one. If you find yourself wondering what is the right thing to do, ask yourself – "If I knew the right thing to do, what would it be?" and *listen* to the response you give yourself.

3. *Put your ego in check.* Before you act, make sure you're not acting from a place of pride, or envy, or doing something because it will make you look good. These are rarely the sources of the "right thing" to do.

4. *Consider the input of others.* Here's a curious technique you might find useful. Do some solo brainstorming by googling quotes on the issue. A client of

mine was once torn about whether to terminate an employee (who probably deserved it), but there were compelling considerations to keep him on the team. She was stuck. She googled "quotes on when to terminate employment" to get fresh ideas. She found three to energize her thinking:

---

*"If you don't get a kick out of the job you're doing, you better kick it and look for another one. Love what you or just don't do it."*

---

*"A successful person continues to look for work after he or she has found it."*

> *"A good rule of thumb is if you've made it to thirty-five and your job still requires you to wear a name tag, you've made a serious vocational error."*

It became clear she was dealing with an individual who was underperforming, perhaps because he was in way over his head. For him, the job had become quite challenging and unfulfilling. That said, he wasn't taking responsibility for improving his situation.

She made her decision, which I won't reveal here. My point is that googling quotes is an unusual, effect way to stimulate your thinking about an issue from a variety of viewpoints.

One more thing: don't forget you can create an imaginary "Board of Directors" – those people you see as mentors or teachers who may have "been there, done that" before you. You don't have to make your decision in isolation. Pick their brains.

> 5. *Ask yourself: if you do the right thing, can you live with the outcome?* Can you look in the mirror and feel good about who you see, when you've chosen the path that's right – especially when it's not the way things are normally done?

Ω   Ω   Ω

If you've found a way forward that will require leadership savvy, not just management skills, act with confidence, conviction, and courage. It may not work out the way you might hope. Doing what's right doesn't come with any guarantees. But then, consider the words of author Tim McMahon: "Risk-taking is inherently failure-prone. Otherwise, it would be called sure-thing-taking."

As you become competent and comfortable being a manager, don't be surprised when you face moments of truth that challenge you to take a risk and be a leader. You can do amazing things, inspire others, and change the world when you take a chance and do the right thing.

# Chapter 7: When I Want Your Opinion

They often say it's lonely at the top.

For one thing, managers often grumble about how difficult it is to think "out loud" in front of their staff because their spoken thoughts are inevitably taken as gospel by subordinates. "I wonder what would happen if we took the less expensive option?" is heard as "The boss wants to cut the budget!"

A story that may be just an urban legend makes the point. It seems the CEO of a multinational organization was conducting an international senior staff meeting discussing global budgets. He was handed a paper-clipped report. Gazing at it, he mused out loud, "I wonder what this corporation spends each year on paper clips?"

A staffer took the question literally, and immediately commissioned a study to determine the answer. Eventually he produced a (stapled, of course) report for the CEO with all the facts and figures about the use of paper clips throughout the organization. The effort to produce the report itself supposedly cost over $10,000.

Thinking out loud can be hazardous to your bottom line!

Secondly, it can be lonely at the top because leaders often have trouble getting "straight talk" from their staff. For many subordinates, the urge to tell the boss what they think he or she wants to hear has become the default position; the idea of being candid with the boss is almost inconceivable.

You can't be effective if the people surrounding you are sugar-coating, obfuscating, or avoiding the unvarnished truth – at least, the truth as they see it. Nearly everyone agrees that you'll be more effective leading people if you can get them to weigh in with a variety of opinions to shape the best path forward.

Let's suppose two of your staff, Janet and Dennis, have been working for about three months on a project – and it's stalled. You've been wondering whether you should give it more resources, or simply pull the plug. You bring it up at a staff meeting, sharing a few observations you'd made. Eventually, you say, "I'd like your opinion on this."

Janet thinks she's heard, "The boss wants to throw even more money on this silly thing."

Dennis would swear he's heard, "The boss wants to kill the project!"

Let's suppose Janet believes the project is not going to work out. She doesn't reveal this. Instead, she says, "We've come a long way, but you're right – it's going to take additional resources to make this thing work."

Dennis actually favors going forward but offers this: "Probably a good idea to kill it, boss. We gave it a good shot, but it's just not working out."

*Both* were offering what they thought you wanted to hear. Not their own opinion, but an echo of what they believed you wanted to do. Not straight-talk, not an honest point of view, and certainly not helpful.

What can you do?

You could pause from having a *content* discussion ("what should we do?"), and have the staff weigh in on the *process* of gathering opinions. You have a teachable moment to exploit!

I witnessed a savvy manager who'd been struggling with this issue. After some reflection, she put together a poster to hang in the staff conference room. It became the first item on the agenda for her next meeting. The poster contained the following:

## When I ask your opinion...

*I want YOUR opinion.*

- I don't want my opinion restated in different words.
- I don't want your "safe" opinion, which doesn't directly contradict my opinion but is nonetheless designed to avoid any conflict between the two of us.
- I don't want the opinion you think I want to hear.

*I want YOUR opinion.*

- I want it because I like to think aloud.

- I want to know whether there are different ways of looking at the issue.
- I want to gauge your understanding.

*I want YOUR opinion.*

- Not because I want to steal your ideas.
- Not because I can't make up my own mind.
- Not because I want to make you feel foolish.

*I want YOUR opinion.*

- I want to sharpen our thinking.
- I want to clarify assumptions – mine and yours.

- I want to discover alternatives, if they exist.
- I want to move the problem-solving forward.

*I want YOUR opinion.*

- Not because I'm *supposed* to ask for the opinions of others.
- Not because I was told to practice "participative management."
- Not because I think you're smarter than me.
- And certainly not because I think I'm smarter than you.

***When I ask your opinion…***

- I won't tell you what it should be. It's *your* opinion and I will value it.
- I hope you'll offer it with honesty and candor. As I do mine.

*That's* how you get people to be straight, candid, and forthcoming. You set the expectations consciously and clearly. You don't leave it to chance.

Until you do this, you'll be dealing with the flotsam created by previous boss-subordinate relationships. We've all worked for a boss who thrived on validation, confirmation and acquiescence. You know the type: "When I want your opinion, I'll tell you what it is."

If you don't want to be lonely at the top, don't be that boss. Instead, be the one who values the opinions of others. Be the one who encourages staff to think, to take the risk of offering a different point of view, to say *out loud* what they truly believe.

If you want straight talk, give them straight talk. Share your expectations. Reward and acknowledge staff when they meet them. Then enjoy the bounty that comes from processing different perspectives.

You'll soon stop complaining it's lonely at the top.

## Chapter 8: Program Your RAS for Success

Have you ever wondered how information that's important to you reaches your conscious mind, while other information is filtered out? For instance, while you consciously attend to the words on this page, odds are you are *not* paying any attention to the amount of pressure your foot feels in its shoe. When you're enjoying the aroma of freshly baked chocolate chip cookies, you're completely unaware of the temperature of the back of your neck.

All of the information about the ways we experience the world, such as sight, smell, touch, sound and so on, is sent to our brain all of the time. These messages are passed through a filter – a group of cells at the base of your brain – before reaching consciousness. There would be no way for you to process everything, at once, all the time. The filter, called your Reticular Activating System (RAS) has the responsibility to determine what gets through to consciousness, and what does not.

Your RAS will also "wake you up" to any threats in your environment. As you read this, most likely you're unaware of any danger. But, if the scent of smoke began wafting into your room, because a spark from the fireplace in another room had blown on the carpet and started to burn, your RAS will alert you immediately and the message, "Something's burning!" will supersede any thoughts you may have about this chapter.

Your RAS is what allows you to focus on what's (currently) important to you and leave the rest in the background. Because you have a RAS, you can drive home from work with a sort of mental "cruise control," absorbed in deep thought, seemingly paying no attention to the road conditions until you suddenly realize it's time to merge to the lane that exits closest to home. On a conscious level, you've been paying *no* attention to the drive, but on a non-conscious level, information about cars breaking, speeding up, or changing lanes ahead of you has been processed the entire time. It's not until a bit of "personally profitable" information emerges – the proper exit is just ahead – that you become aware once again of all this data.

These are the two operating principles of the RAS:

> 1. All information that is sent toward the brain, from all the sensory organs, is allowed to pass into consciousness if any of it

represents danger or a threat.

2. Any information that is "personally profitable" will also pass through the RAS as conscious thought. Personally profitable information is that which sustains a belief we hold to be true.

Without getting too deep in the weeds, beliefs are simply things we hold to be true about the world around us – whether or not they are objectively true. The strongest of these formed in childhood when we are told by much larger human beings what's true and what isn't.

- You're such a good girl!
- You're such a precocious girl!
- That's a *great* picture. I love how you did this!

- That's not how it's done. You must color within the lines – and trees aren't purple, for heaven's sake!

- If you work hard, like your father, and his father before him, you'll have a home of your own one day.

- If you don't fight for everything you want, like your father and his father before him, you'll never have a home of your own one day.

Statements like these, pounded day after day onto the blank canvas of a child's mind, become strongly held and largely non-conscious beliefs – and program the RAS to understand what's personally profitable information – anything that "proves" the belief is true.

If you believe something is true, you will literally see evidence of it everywhere. Likewise, if you don't believe it, you'll walk by a clear example of it and see nothing of the kind.

Participants in a workshop were sent out of the classroom into the environment for twenty minutes, asked to gather observations in support of a statement they were to pretend they believed to be true (whether they did or not in actual life). The statement whispered to them might be one of the following:

- Generally speaking, people are rather generous, or
- Generally speaking, people are rather stingy

When they returned, people looking for generosity reported noticing a person who gave up a parking space for another, someone who allowed a mother with a baby carriage to move ahead of them in line, or someone going out of her way to pick up a piece of trash and discard it.

Those looking for stinginess noticed the person who cut off a driver to secure a parking place, or the one who put money in a newspaper dispenser and withdrew two papers, or someone who wouldn't pause to help them with directions.

What's most interesting, is that neither group even saw what the other group saw. None of the "generous" group saw the driver cutting off another for a parking space, and none of the "stingy" group saw the person who let a mother ahead of him in line.

Through our RAS, *we see what we expect to see.* We see what's personally profitable – any evidence that what we believe to be true is actually true.

## People will rise or fall to your level of expectations

If you expect (believe) that someone will perform well and meet or exceed your standards, chances are good you'll be right.

Why? Because you will *notice* when they're doing well, and reward that behavior with public or private praise, encouraging them to tackle tough assignments, start offering them more challenging projects, and the like. You won't even notice the times when they miss the mark, come in late, or become grumpy with a customer.

If you expect (believe) that someone will perform poorly and not meet your standards, chances are good you're right. You'll *notice* when they do poorly, and deliver consequences that might include anything from a deep sigh and rolling eyes, to reassignment on an easier project, to an unsatisfactory performance review.

## Let's consider an example

Imagine you supervise a department where the work has typically and historically been done by one gender or the other. You learn you're about to receive a transfer employee whom you've never met – Dana. What you've been told about Dana is fairly straightforward and positive. There are no red flags whatsoever. The position has been open awhile and you're eager for Dana to start. On the first day, Dana shows up and – surprise! – Dana is a (fill in the gender). Not at all what you expected. Dana looks like, talks like, and in fact is the kind of person who rarely succeeds in this line of work.

Without your conscious awareness, your RAS kicks in, and begins to look for evidence that your belief – people of this gender never do well in this line of work. What will you likely see almost immediately?

- You'll notice any gaps in Dana's technical knowledge
- You'll observe any way in which Dana doesn't fit in with the rest of the team
- You'll fret whenever Dana does something differently than it's been done in the past
- You'll shudder when Dana makes a mistake

Eventually, if your RAS is unchecked, your prediction will come true. Dana just won't cut it. It's almost like the handwriting was on the wall on Dana's first day. Dana fails.

Are we to conclude that if Dana fails, it's because of you? Of course not – but there's an element of the scenario that you can own and do differently if you want. You can program your RAS to change what's personally profitable. If you realize you have a deep-seated belief about whether men or women can be successful in your line of work, you can change it. You can begin to affirm a *new* belief and, just as the participants in the workshop discovered, find evidence that it is also true in the larger world.

You can say to yourself:

- These days, anyone can do this work
- Given a real chance, Dana can thrive here

- When I look at Dana, I see lots of examples of clear competence, initiative and professionalism

Ω   Ω   Ω

As you make a *conscious* effort to reprogram your RAS, you will notice real-world "proof" that these new beliefs are true. You will notice when Dana tackles a problem with creativity, or stays a little longer one day to make sure an assignment is complete, or joshes with a co-worker and gets a laugh.

Dana will make it – or not – based on many factors: competence, aptitude, and frankly a bit of luck. Only you, as Dana's boss, can program your RAS to see Dana succeed. Do you want to be a factor in a story of achievement or one of disappointment?

## Chapter 9: Three Words Leaders Hesitate to Say

There are three little words which, when formed as a sentence, have the power to bring some managers to their knees. Rather than utter them out loud, they'll avoid them, change the subject, or quickly move on.

The words: "I don't know."

Let's talk about Tom, for example, whom you first met in Chapter Three. He's the fellow whose X-Factor was decisiveness – in spades. He *never* sat on the fence.

That said, he also had another characteristic that wasn't always admired by his staff. He wasn't, by anyone's standards, a very good listener. If you came to him with a problem, for instance, he'd be on the phone calling someone (to resolve the issue) before you could complete your third sentence. If you were looking for an empathetic ear, you had to look elsewhere. It was long after I worked for Tom that I learned that his passion for taking immediate action (instead of active listening) was his way of hiding a secret.

Years after we'd gone our separate ways, we were reminiscing about our time together. I asked Tom why he had such an impulse to leap into the fray rather than engage in mutual problem-solving or simply letting people vent.

He gave that some thought. "I'm not sure who taught me this – perhaps it was my father – but I grew up believing that the boss – or anyone in authority, was someone who was supposed to know what to do, who to call, or how to solve the problem," he said. "*Any* problem.

"I grew up wanting to be that person."

When he became a manager, he realized the worst situation he could envision would be getting caught not knowing what to do about an issue. He shuddered when he imagined himself having to say out loud, "I don't know." It would show weakness and make him vulnerable. It would be a moment of failure.

"But there must have been times, Tom," I said, "when you truly were stumped. When you didn't have enough information, or experience, or even intuition to know what to do."

"Oh, there were many times. No doubt about that."

"How did you handle it?" I asked.

"I would do anything *that looked like* I knew the answer. Sometimes I'd challenge the question. Or I'd change the subject. My first impulse, most of the time, was to take action – any action. Looking back, I cannot remember a single time when I would simply say, 'I don't know.' At the time, I saw that as a sign of strength. It took me many years to recognize my folly."

Tom wasn't exceptional in his organization in that regard, nor much different from many leaders elsewhere. Remember, people like Tom are admired, praised, and compensated for being smart – for knowing all the answers. They are often promoted to leadership positions precisely because of their reputation of knowing what to do, regardless of the issue. They support a leadership paradigm whose foundation is the idea that the boss is the one who knows more than anyone in the room. For people like Tom, admitting they don't know something is to be weak and vulnerable.

"We are told that leaders must be strong. They must be confident. They must be unflinching. They must hide their fear. They must never blink. They cannot be soft in any way. I call bullshit," says Brad Feld, a successful software developer.

He's right. A strong, effective leader is the one who is willing to say, when necessary, "I don't know." But there's much more to it.

## Saying "I don't know" is only half the story.

Being a manager sometimes can feel like you spend your time dealing with a series of interruptions, interrupted by other interruptions. Employees are constantly grabbing our attention to get answers to their pressing concerns, like:

- Will this project be successful if we change the milestones?
- Do you think this product feature will attract enough new customers?

- Are they going to slash our budget again?
- Any news on a fix to the overtime problem?
- Why is Trudy taking so long to get us the figures?
- How long will we have to wait to fill Gene's position?

When they do, sometimes you'll realize the only honest answer is "I don't know." If you're like Tom, you could easily feel stuck. Your impulse will be to dodge the question.

Effective leaders know it's important to be candid and open with their staff by revealing when they can't answer a question, *and* they know admitting they don't know is only half the solution. They know the importance of taking the question to another level. They say things like:

- "I don't know, but I'll find out and let you know."
- "I don't know, but my best guess is..."
- "I don't know; we should probably ask [name]..."
- "I don't know much about that, but here's what I can tell you."
- "I don't know – that's exactly what I'm trying to find out."
- "I don't know – thanks for asking. Let me look into that."
- "I don't know – that's a really good question. Let me find out."

- "I don't know – and here's why I don't know."

Pretty subtle, that's for sure. (Chapter 14, "Get Off Your Butt," and Chapter 15, "The 16 Seconds of Silence" explore two powerful communication techniques that are quite simple and based on common sense. That said, common sense isn't often common practice.)

Think of it as a three-step process:

1. Admit (to yourself) that you can't answer the question.
2. Admit (to the questioner) that you don't know.
3. Continue to *lead* by suggesting the next step.

The problem for leaders like Tom is they get stuck on the first step. They can't accept that they're infallible, human, and not all-knowing. They don't realize (or believe) that honesty and vulnerability actually strengthen the admiration their staff will have for them. They can't get to Step Three because they can't take Step One or Two.

Become a manager who's willing to say, "I don't know" with a clear follow-up and you will reap two benefits:

1. You'll be seen as a leader who's willing to tell the truth, even when it could be embarrassing or difficult. This will encourage your staff, in turn, to tell the truth.

2. You'll avoid the fallout that can come from pretending to know what you don't know. Experience tells us that the odds are good everyone knows when you

don't know. You're rarely fooling anyone.

Ω    Ω    Ω

When Tom was asked if there was anything he'd do differently as a leader if he had it to do over, he grew thoughtful for a moment, and then smiled.

"I don't know," he said. "But I'm looking into that and I'll get back to you!"

## Chapter 10: Give 'em the Kool-Aid

One of the most important challenges for a leader is to help your people align their personal self-interest with that of the organization. When done well, magic starts to happen.

Early in my career, I was a humble "outside" sales person working for a furniture rental company. There was nothing particularly sexy about my job – I spent my day traveling from one apartment complex to another, visiting with the apartment manager with the aim of getting her to mention our company's name to new tenants when they lacked furniture of their own. I refreshed a brochure stand, gave the manager a free scratch pad or two, and made some small talk. My goal was to get 20-30 referrals a month from my territory, which could be translated into new customers by our team of "inside" sales people on the showroom floor.

The sales staff had the good fortune to work for a sales manager named Sally, who became my mentor and inspiration for many years to come. You met Sally in Chapter Three, when you learned about her X-Factor – positivity.

Sally was by far the most positive person I've ever known. She didn't *talk* about the importance of staying positive; she *lived* it. Example: she literally refused to accept the word "problem" if it came up in conversation. If you came to her saying, "Sally, there's a problem with a delivery to the Ridgeview Apartments (meaning, for example, the delivery was late)," she would ignore you.

It took a while for newer employees to understand that the approach had to be, "Sally, there's an *opportunity* with a delivery to the Ridgeview Apartments." Said that way, she would give you her instant, complete attention. Then you could tell her the delivery was late.

See the difference between problems and opportunities? Problems are negative; opportunities are positive. Problems give us headaches; opportunities give us energy. Problems are things to avoid; opportunities are things to embrace. Problems lead to blame; opportunities lead to solutions. Sally's staff *never* had problems, they had opportunities!

Having a boss like Sally can come as a shock. Can you imagine a boss who always sees the glass as half full?

Her positivity was infectious. She didn't turn everyone around right away, but after time, every member of the team developed an optimistic, enthusiastic attitude and work ethic. Positivity was not only her X-Factor, it was her Kool-Aid.

As we drank Sally's Kool-Aid, there came a time where we cared so much about our work that we found time to meet on our own, after work, to figure out ways we could help each other. I doubt Sally ever knew – though she wouldn't have been surprised. We became obsessed with furniture rental, of all things, and began to see ourselves as "missionaries" on a quest to put rental furniture in every apartment. We set company records month after month, and quite a few of the team rose to much higher levels in the organization.

## An astronomical impact

I had the opportunity to accompany an astronaut touring an electronics company that supplied parts to manned rockets and other space vehicles. At one point, he paused in front of a group of assemblers, most of whom spoke English only as a second language, and asked them, "Do you know what this thing (the part they made) actually does?"

Not a hand went up. Not a single assembler knew. They only knew that they took some parts they got from that department over there and assembled something that got passed to a department down the hall. What the thing did, and why it mattered, was something they knew nothing about.

The astronaut served up some Kool-Aid immediately: "This part," he said seriously, "literally keeps me alive." Then, in some detail, he explained how. You could have heard a pin drop. He concluded by thanking the assemblers for their attention to detail and continued his tour.

A few weeks later, I spoke with the supervisor of that department. He was astonished, he revealed, at what happened following the tour. He reported that *every* measure of productivity and quality went up since the tour, and he attributed it *all* to the astronaut's visit. Perhaps unconsciously, the astronaut had linked the assemblers' self-interest (pride in doing a good job) to the organization's self-interest (producing the highest quality electronic parts for space vehicles). What they did no longer was a simple matter of putting parts together – it was a matter of life-and-death for real people. They had never thought of it that way before.

## Camping in the park

A few years ago, I found myself walking through a park in San Diego, enjoying the beautiful trees, lawns, and view of the ocean. Lost in my own reverie, I didn't notice the city tree trimmer at first.

"Did you know," he said, coming up to me, "that you can camp in this park?"

No, I didn't. Hadn't even occurred to me. He began to explain how one goes about camping in the park, and his enthusiasm was unmistakable. His pride in "his" park was contagious, and I asked him where I could get more information. He wrote down a website address. Afterwards, I realized I'd never seen an unassuming tree trimmer acting as an enthusiastic ambassador for the parks, but there he was. He was not just a tree trimmer. He was someone creating places for people to enjoy overnight camping much closer to home.

I couldn't help but conclude that someone had given him some Kool-Aid, and that he had enjoyed a glass or two.

# What's this Kool-Aid of which I speak?

Sometimes it's called the *vision*. Sometimes it's called the *mission*. It's the rationale for the organization, expressed in a way that helps people connect what's near and dear to *them* with something larger and even more important.

The manager of Parks and Recreation for a small city in northern California made it his practice to tell people the reason his department existed was to *create joy* for citizens who lived there. On paper, it was worded differently: their task to build and maintain parks, coordinate outdoor activities ranging from Little League to the annual Corn Fest parade, and so on.

But whether his employees were mowing a lawn, publishing the soccer league schedule, or submitting a requisition for new pool equipment, they knew the reason they did what they did was to create joy for people. They were cheerful, committed, engaged employees. *Creating joy* was their Kool-Aid.

## What's *your* Kool-Aid?

Here's something to think about: what's the Kool-Aid for *your* team? What's the higher purpose, the compelling reason you and your people do what they do? Why do you and your folks get up in the morning? If you want them to aspire to remarkable achievement, it has to be more than just getting the job done. It has to be more than earning a paycheck. It has to really mean something. It has to matter.

Here's a simple technique to discover what's truly important. Ask yourself these questions (with example responses):

1. What does your department do?
*We create financial reports for City Council.*

2. Why is *that* important?
*Council uses these reports to make sound financial decisions.*

3. Why is *that* important?
*These decisions impact every citizen in the city.*

4. Why is *that* important?
*Everyone wants the most livable city possible.*

5. Why is *that* important?
*A "livable" city is what makes living here so enjoyable.*

See it? *That's* the Kool-Aid. "We create financial reports, paying enormous attention to detail, double- and triple-checking our work for accuracy, to enable City Council to make good financial decisions which will result in the most livable city we can imagine."

What's yours?

# Chapter 11: The More Things Change

Nearly everyone agrees that the world is changing at a faster clip than ever. The specific rate of change may be hard to calculate, but consider this:

- We've had human speech for 10,000 generations
- Agriculture for 750
- Writing for 500
- Universities for 40
- Printing for 24
- Telephones for 5
- Radio for 4
- Television for 3
- Computers for 2, and
- The internet for *one* generation

Or this:

- It took YouTube four years to have 50 million users
- It took Facebook three
- It took Twitter two
- It took the game Angry Birds *35 days* to reach that mark

Inventor and futurist Ray Kurzweil wrote on his blog (http://www.kurzweilai.net/blog), "It is not the case that we will experience a hundred years of progress in the twenty-first century; rather, we will witness on the order of twenty thousand years of progress (at today's rate of progress, that is)." A commenter responded, "the human brain is, after all, also a computer about 100,000 times more powerful than the typical desktop [computer] today. But today's desktop is 100,000 times more powerful than the equivalent computer just 25 years ago."

What *hasn't* changed, however, is our human capacity to absorb and integrate change. We still do it the same way as our ancestors did – except now, we have much more to handle.

On the practical level, how will your staff react to changes like these?

- There's a new process for requisitioning tools
- Sandy has announced she'll be leaving, and Taylor will (temporarily) be assuming her responsibilities
- We're bumping up the project schedule for the new McMaster deliverable

- Brian has been asked to deliver his first-ever presentation with a client
- The division director wants us to computerize our status reports

Knowing how people typically react to change is vitally important, because you can minimize (or at least be prepared for) any resistance that might arise.

By the way, many people believe that people resist change, almost universally and automatically. It's almost a cliché. If you're going to introduce something new to your staff – whatever it is – they're going to resist it. Prepare yourself! While there is *some* truth to this chestnut, it is more accurate to say people resist *being* changed.

Suppose you develop a curiosity about playing golf. Looks like it might be fun; might be a sublime way to relax outdoors on the weekends. Given this interest, you start visiting sporting goods stores, taking yourself to driving ranges, arranging for a few lessons, and perhaps even investing in some equipment. You as a golfer? Big change. Resistance? None.

Now imagine your boss comes to you and suggests you take up golf, out of the blue. "It'll be a good career move," he says. "Lots of deals get made on the golf course. I'd strongly suggest you take it up." In this scenario: You don't like golf. You actually *hate* golf. On top of that, you detest the idea of having to conduct business this way. You'll probably strongly resist taking up the sport. You don't need to be anxious about leading a change effort at work. You need to be forearmed! How will people actually react, and what should you do about that?

A clever workshop activity created by Ken Blanchard, widely known for his book,

*The One Minute Manager*) illustrates what he calls the seven "human dynamics" of change. According to Blanchard, when a group of people, like those on your team, must make a change (a new process, a new team member, altered priorities, new software and so forth) they will predictably demonstrate all seven.

## The "Change" Exercise

The exercise begins with participants being asked to stand up, mill about, and find a partner. Once they've done that, they should stand facing each other. At that point, Ken asks them to take about twenty seconds to "memorize" their partner's appearance (in silence). Then, they are asked to turn back-to-back and alter their own appearance in five ways (again, in silence). They are to simply make themselves look different.

People begin removing jewelry, loosening their tie, taking off a name badge and so on. After a few moments, they are asked to face each other once again and take turns seeing if they can tell what's different about their partner's appearance.

Next, they are asked to turn back-to-back a second time. Now, he says, they are to make *ten* additional changes to their own appearance – in addition to the first five. Typically, there's lots of nervous laughter in the air. "You've got to be kidding!" and "There's no way!" are among the responses.

Regardless, Ken urges them to do their best, and participants give it a go. They are asked to face each other once again and see if they can pick out the new alterations.

At last, Ken has them thank their partner and return to their seats. If you were watching, you'd notice that most of them put everything (jewelry, shoes, nametags, etc.) back in their original place before the exercise.

## The Debrief – the Seven Dynamics

Here are the seven dynamics revealed by the exercise. Note: not everyone exhibits every dynamic, but with a group, the odds are great that at least *someone* will experience each one.

*1. Feeling awkward or ill-at ease.*

Nearly everyone reports that when instructed to silently memorize their partner's appearance, they felt uncomfortable. Some of it is social conditioning – after all, we are not "supposed" to stare at another person. This dynamic is also a typical reaction to *any* change. We feel discomfort, at first, when we're asked to do something new or in a different way.

2. *People will probably ask themselves, "What do I have to give up?"*

How do we know this? Because, in the exercise, nearly everyone "subtracted" from their appearance. They removed watches, rings, nametags, shoes. They "gave things up." Almost no one changed their appearance by adding a jacket or a pen, for example.

3. *Many felt overwhelmed.*

In the middle of the exercise, asked to make ten additional changes – not two, or three or so – many people report afterwards feeling overwhelmed at that point. Some have even dropped out and returned to their seat.

*4. Many people remember feeling they lacked the resources to do what was asked.*

During the debrief, they would joke that they hadn't worn enough layers of clothing to make these changes. Or they felt stumped – perhaps they weren't smart enough to comply with the instruction. (In real-life situations, you might hear people grumble they don't have enough time, or budget, or training, or experience, or tools to make a change. These are all versions of "I don't have enough resources.")

*5. Some folks talked about feeling isolated and alone in the midst of the exercise.*

Without thinking about it, most believed that they had to figure out the exercise instructions all by themselves. They largely avoided eye contact with (or even looking around the room at) other participants. They worked out what they'd do by themselves, rarely borrowing a good idea from someone else.

6. *People were at different levels of readiness to make changes.*

Some were quickly at an impasse ("Ten more?"), while others were ready for yet *another* round of change-making. You see that when you watch people adopt new technology. At one end of a continuum are the "early adopters" (the first to try a new device), while at the other end are the "laggards" (the last to get on board).

7. *At the end of the activity participants often reverted back to their original appearance.*

How often have you seen that in your own experience of change? Something is introduced, the group struggles for a while, and when the heat is off, they return to the old pattern.

In one organization when email (replacing the interoffice memo) was first introduced (yes, there was a time before email!), the rationale was to save paper. It was a fundamental, sweeping, and for many people frightening change. Employees ranged from the eager to the frozen. Many feared they would lose their memos in cyberspace, where, for all they know, they might be irretrievable. To assuage their own worries, they *reverted back to the ways things worked before*. They *printed* all their outgoing and incoming emails. After the first year, a quick study revealed that paper costs hadn't diminished at all.

# Applying the lessons of the exercise

What can you take from this exercise? How can you manage a change initiative – starting a new schedule, adhering to a new policy, refining a process, on-boarding a new employee, or introducing new technology? Here's seven suggestions:

1. *Help your staff feel less awkward or ill-at-ease* in the beginning by simply acknowledging that they are probably going to feel awkward. It's a funny thing: when we're given "permission" to feel uncomfortable, we feel it less strongly.

2. Remember learning to drive a car with a standard transmission? It would have been ideal if your instructor had said, "I want you to place your hands on the

steering wheel. In a moment, you're going to use your right hand (or left, depending on where you live) to operate the shift lever, your right foot to depress the accelerator, and your left foot to operate the brake *and* clutch pedal, while keeping your left hand on the steering wheel. It's going to feel a bit overwhelming at first – but you'll soon get the hang of it." *Remind people that at first, everything will seem complicated and take more time than it used to. Encourage them to trust that with time, just like learning to drive a standard transmission automobile, the new way will become natural.*

3. If you have the sense that at least some members of your staff will be wondering what they're going to have to give up as a result of the change ("New schedule,

huh? I'm not going to get Thursday mornings off now?") *identify and acknowledge those losses immediately – and then shift the focus on what's to be gained* ("Yes, that's correct. But you're also going to be working one less Saturday a month with the new schedule.")

4. People often feel overwhelmed with change ("Now make ten additional changes to your appearance.") when they perceive the new thing as too much, or too soon. *Can you break down the required changes into smaller steps?* ("Make one more change in your appearance. Excellent! Now make one more. Good! Now another.") Remember, too, that the change you're asking people to embrace is (for them) connected to everything else they're being asked to

change, both at work and in their personal life. What might look like a small change in the office can be overwhelming when they're dealing with a plateful of other things. Acknowledgement and empathy go a long way in this circumstance.

5. If you're hearing they don't have the resources, consider – *can you help provide them*? Can you give them tools, tutorials, formal training, or even a relaxed change management project schedule?

6. *Address feelings of isolation* with candid team meetings where people can express their concerns and hear from others how they're managing the change effort.

7. Finally, if you have people spanning the spectrum from early adopters to laggards, *put them together*! Let those who are embracing the change work with and inspire those who have concerns.

Ω   Ω   Ω

It's up to you. Address the natural, predictable, very human dynamics of change, or brace yourself for people to struggle with the changes you introduce. If you support your staff through the uncomfortable stages of change you will greatly improve the odds, and reduce the time it takes, for successful implementation of the change.

Embrace change. Befriend it. Learn the ways of change. As the Greek philosopher Heraclitus said, "There is nothing permanent except change."

# Section Three: Communication

By far, the biggest complaints about organizations have to do with communication. In my experience with over 300 clients, when employees are asked the *most important* thing that needs improvement where they work, the answer is invariably *communication*. By that they may mean different things, such as a request for more communication from the top, or a complaint that there's too many emails, or a request for an improved way to deliver performance feedback to subordinates. One lamented, "I never know whether to send my boss a text, a voice mail, an email, or just drop by when I've got something important to share."

Communication is a "fat" word – it can mean so many things!

In this section, we'll focus on some practical communication issues:

- Comparing how highly effective and not-so-effective leaders speak with staff

- Improving the quality of your feedback to others

- Getting people who are reluctant to speak up to do just that

- Putting an end to conversations that seem to go 'round and 'round without getting anywhere

# Chapter 12: How Effective Leaders Talk

Have you dined at Benihana? The Japanese restaurant chain (with over 70 locations nationwide) is famous for preparing its food in full view of the patrons, with a panache that gives new meaning to the phrase "dinner theatre."

Chefs amuse and delight you juggling their spatulas and knives. Their amazing culinary repertoire is on full display as they grill the food, balancing many different orders simultaneously. Then, with uncanny accuracy they stun patrons by sending food flying from the grill directly to your plate – or even your mouth! While the food is good, fully immersing customers in the preparation and presentation experience is what separates Benihana from conventional restaurants.

Effective leaders remind me of Benihana chefs. They too have mastered a set of skills that they make look effortless. In particular, their communication skills. These folks know how to inspire us, teach us something new, pat us on the back, or make a course correction in ways that create a sense of connection – whether it's between us and them, or us and a vision. Experts have noted these effective leaders have a knack of reducing complex ideas into bite-sized chunks (no pun intended) that nearly anyone can understand, without over-simplifying the message.

When effective leaders communicate well, they earn our respect and loyalty. They motivate us to try harder, work smarter, and "make it so."

By the way, this is not a chapter about famous leadership quotes from people like: Abraham Lincoln: "No man has a good enough memory to be a successful liar," or

John F. Kennedy: "Ask not what your country can do for you; ask what you can do for your country," or even Winston Churchill: "Success consists of going from failure to failure without loss of enthusiasm." This is about how *ordinary* (but actually extraordinary) leaders in everyday situations *talk* with their teams, from the sales manager to the maintenance supervisor to the vice president of finance to the school superintendent, in organizations across the land.

I've been collecting comments from leaders like these for years. Here's some examples that are great models for anyone striving to take a leadership practice to another level:

---

*"This is excellent work. I especially liked the summary. You nailed it!*

---

The boss has "caught someone doing something right" (something effective leaders do often). Her comment is brief, specific, and enthusiastic. She knows that what gets rewarded (even by an "attaboy") tends to get repeated.

---

*"You're a valuable member of this team."*

---

Who wouldn't want to hear this from time to time? It conveys appreciation. It costs nothing to say, but could pay big dividends. "You're a valuable member of this team" should *not* go without saying.

---

*"Help me understand how you reached your conclusion. What are your underlying assumptions?"*

---

This manager resisted any impulse he might have had to ridicule the idea (or the employee), knowing that by demonstrating respect for his subordinate, he increases the strength of connection. The manager is also smart enough to know that he doesn't know everything. By collaborating, there's a good chance the two of them will reach a conclusion they can both support.

---

*"I don't yet agree with your position, but I appreciate you offering a different perspective. Good food for thought."*

---

It costs the leader nothing to acknowledge and appreciate different points of view. She's honest ("I don't yet agree with your position.") without being condescending or authoritative. The odds are high that the conversation will continue and go deeper.

- "I can see how you feel stuck between the policy and your sense of what the right thing to do is. Where do you think we should go from here?"

How empowering! The leader recognizes that the employee has a genuine dilemma. Perhaps they can figure out the next steps together. No preaching, no telling the employee what to do. The leader may actually know (or believe) there's a "best path" forward, but when he puts it this way, he opens the door to a genuine dialogue that might even lead to "teachable moments" that would otherwise have been overlooked.

> *"What resources do you need to complete this project?"*

This is what we call an *open-ended* question. Here's a few more:

"What happened after the meeting?"
"Why did Jack stay late?"
"How did the presentation go?"

Compare those with these *closed-ended* questions:

"Was it a good meeting?"
"Did Jack stay late?"
"Any problems with the presentation?"

There is almost no way to respond to an open-ended question with just one or two words. Open-ended questions are the stockin-trade for effective leaders, because they *encourage* conversation. They require the listener to think about how to respond. With a question like "What resources do you need to complete this project?" the boss is signaling a willingness to listen, a genuine curiosity, and a respect for the employee who is probably in a far better position to know what resources are needed.

---

*"Let me do a listening check. It sounds like you're saying..."*

---

Please: *memorize* that sentence and use it often. "Let me do a listening check." This is neutral; it is not a thinly disguised version of "You're not making any sense!" It's a simple pause in the ebb-and-flow of the conversation to ensure that both parties are on the same page. It's respectful and useful. It allows the employee to respond with an affirmation: "Yes, that's what I mean..." *or* a clarification: "No, what I meant was..." without risking losing face.

---

*"That must have taken some courage to tell me. Thanks."*

---

Recognizing what's not being said is as critical as understanding what is. Suppose Hank was offering his boss some feedback following the boss's presentation at a cross-functional team meeting, and further suppose he had some ideas on how that presentation might be improved. If Hank's boss wants to get honest, direct feedback, she needs to acknowledge and reward the effort (remember, what gets rewarded gets repeated). Recognizing Hank's courage wouldn't even occur to most managers; highly effective leaders spot it immediately and thank him for his straight talk.

---

*"I can't give you my full attention right now, and that's not fair to you. Let's schedule a time that's good for both of us."*

---

The key phrase here is, *"and that's not fair to you."* Here's a boss who is aware of his own situation, and the impact of that situation on the employee. A less-aware supervisor would have simply said, "I can't give you my full attention right now; let's reschedule." See the difference?

---

*"How are things, generally speaking? How are you doing?"*

Did you recognize the open-ended question? What's at play here is what's called a "check-in." It's the boss taking a conscious action to connect with her subordinate. It should be done regularly but without predictability. It shows that you care about the employee. Remember the old saw? *"Nobody cares how much you know until they know how much you care."* If you want your followers' respect, demonstrate that you care about them.

---

*"I've interrupted you. Please continue."*

---

Here's a leader demonstrating self-awareness, vulnerability, and respect for the other. Admitting your own flaws, without wallowing in them, is a reliable way to connect with others. You're fully human and able to admit it.

*"When we add this assignment to your plate, what will need to come off?"*

Too many people work for supervisors or managers who swear by the shopworn phrase, "We need to do more with less." A good leader *knows* that you can't add tasks and assignments indefinitely without some being downgraded or eliminated. Of course, it's also another great open-ended question.

*"Next time, what could you have done differently? What could I do differently?"*

This is a leader who knows the value of debriefing after an activity. The word "differently" is the key here, and it's chosen deliberately, instead of the word "better." It's neutral. It's likely to produce less defensiveness.

## *"Do you feel heard?"*

There's some fascinating research about what people think are the most important qualities for a boss. A wide cross-section of employees in many walks of life were asked to make their wish list of attributes their ideal supervisor should have. As you might expect, a few things came up repeatedly, such as good technical knowledge, being approachable, being a "people-person," and others.

When the lists of thousands of people were collapsed into one aggregate list, one item rose to the top: "I'd like to work for a person who gave me the experience of *being heard.*" Someone who convinces me they have listened; they've given it real thought; they can paraphrase it back to me in a way that demonstrates they really got what I'm saying."

It might very well be the *most important* characteristic of the ideal boss.

A leader who remembers to ask, "Do you feel heard?" is going a long way to creating that experience for those fortunate enough to be on his team. "I know that you believe you understand what you think I said, but I'm not sure you realize that what you heard is not what I meant," goes the famous quote from Robert McCloskey, the well-known children's writer and illustrator. Far simpler is to ask, now and then, "Do you feel heard?"

---

*"I'm pretty sure this will feel like an unreasonable request, and I wish I didn't have to make it. Let's talk about why I'm asking you to do this."*

---

Empathy. Successful leaders are those who have, and freely share, their empathy for others. A more typical manager might have said, "I need you to work Saturday. Plan to be here by 8 a.m." The first approach described above is likely to produce willingness and perhaps even a sense of commitment; the second brings simple compliance. Which would you rather have?

---

*"It's a pleasure having you as a colleague."*

---

This comment conveys both appreciation *and* respect. Every member of the team has value, and *all* are colleagues, not boss and subordinates. Tell them from time to time.

---

*"You've been putting in a lot of long hours lately. What can we do to restore a sense of life balance?"*

---

When my boss said this to me at a time when I felt overwhelmed, frustrated, and exhausted, I was nearly in shock. At that moment, my work life was an endless and stressful To Do list, and I was starting to feel like an automaton. When she pulled me aside to offer this comment, I felt a relief and hope. I also felt *connected* to her and knew we would begin problem-solving. She *understood* me. She *validated* me.

---

*"It feels good to know I can rely on you."*

---

See a pattern here? Recognition and validation in just ten words. Strong leaders don't hesitate saying things like this – often.

*"What's the lesson we can take from this experience?"*

Another open-ended question. A terrific prompt to fix a problem (if there was one), rather than to find blame. The leader is clearly open to an honest debrief of the situation.

*"I know you didn't agree with this decision, and I'm especially grateful that you gave it your full support after it was made."*

Asking people to get on board regarding a decision might seem routine. The effective leader is one who recognizes that when a staff member supports a decision they didn't agree with, this is an especially valuable contribution, and she makes sure the staffer knows she noticed it and how she feels about it.

> *"I've got some ideas on how you might proceed, and I want to hear yours as well. How about you go first?"*

When the boss goes first, others might not be candid, preferring to say what they think their manager wants to hear. This comment removes this temptation by letting the leader keep his thoughts on the subject private until others have weighed in.

Ω Ω Ω

The Benihana chef wasn't born with spectacular spatula and knife skills. He was mentored; he practiced endlessly, and there can be no doubt he made many mistakes. Eventually, he became a master of his craft. The craft of personal communication is no different. You too can learn to master it and use these skills to lead others to achieve their potential.

Let's take this one step further. The *most important* thing you can do – bar none – to develop as a manager is to become an increasingly more skilled communicator.

# Chapter 13: How Ineffective Leaders Talk

If you've read the last chapter, you've been thinking about some of the things highly effective leaders say. Now let's look at the other side – the things *ineffective* leaders say all too frequently. I've been collecting this list for years. All of the examples are real. The speaker's thoughts (in parentheses), however, are what I imagine them to be.

---

*"If I want your opinion I'll tell you what it is."*

---

Perhaps this is an attempt at humor. Even so, it fails miserably. The so-called joke is a subtle reminder that the boss has the upper hand and most of the power in this relationship. It puts the receiver in her place. It makes it clear that the boss has a higher opinion of himself than of the employee. It's devaluing, demeaning, and – perhaps most importantly – it's simply not true. The employee's opinion belongs to the employee, whether it happens to be the same as her boss's or not. It's not a comment which will inspire straight talk or contribution.

---

*"Since you didn't say anything I have to assume you agreed."*

---

At a meeting, seven people, including their manager, sat around a round conference table struggling to reach consensus on which vendor to choose for an upcoming project. The conversation went back and forth, round and round, and the boss grew increasingly impatient. Finally, she could take no more.

She stood up and pounded her fist on the table. "I think we should pick Vendor A!" she nearly yelled, adding, "Do any of you have a problem with that?"

Her team went silent, and everyone avoided eye contact.

"Good," she said. "We have consensus!"

In a word, no. She didn't have consensus; she had *silence*. It's a safe bet that those meeting participants would later sabotage this decision with gossip or malicious compliance. She had bullied them into *acting as though* they supported the decision.

You've heard it before – don't assume. And if you do, check it out. There's a chance your assumption is incorrect.

---

*"You're paid to do what you're told, not think."*

---

How demoralizing!

Organizations purchase tools and equipment, from screwdrivers to high-speed computers, to *do* things. We don't expect them to think – even modern computers can only "think" as well as they're programmed by people.

Effective leaders expect and encourage employees to think, to develop judgment, and to make decisions based on their experience and training. If someone has committed an error in judgment, the incident becomes a "coachable moment," not a time for talking with someone as though they're a child.

---

*"Who's the idiot who came up with that idea?"*

---

A colleague of mine worked as a unit manager reporting to a director. He was asked to represent his director, who was unable to attend, at the weekly staff meeting held by the general manager. During the meeting, a proposal was put up for discussion, which had been created by Denny.

The GM clearly didn't like the idea, and loudly harrumphed, "Who's the idiot who came up with that idea?" Attending his first GM staff meeting ever, Denny slowly raised his hand and said, "That would be me, sir." His chagrin was palpable.

There is no place whatsoever for language that is insulting, disrespectful, or rude.

---

*"You should be a little more grateful that you even have this job."*

---

For starters, comments that begin with "You should feel…" are almost always a mistake. "You should be glad we…" or "You shouldn't be so upset, given that we…" or "You should be pleased that…" are almost always an unforced error by a leader. Make it your habit to avoid proclaiming how a person *ought* to feel. What you should aim for is helping someone clarify exactly what they *do* feel to the point they're comfortable sharing that insight with you.

When that happens, you can have a conversation in which the other person genuinely feels heard, which in turn makes it more likely they will continue the conversation. Notice the difference between, "You shouldn't be so upset, given that we've changed that policy" with "It looks like you're still upset, even after we've changed the policy." Don't tell someone how they should feel. Seek to understand how they *do* feel.

> *"That is a top priority." (As is everything else you are assigned to do.)*

Like everyone else on the planet, employees develop a BS meter over time. When they hear something is a top priority, and they've grown accustomed to hearing *everything* is a top priority, they start tuning that out. They know it's simply not true. They know it's "boss-speak," not a real conversation.

"When everything is a priority, *nothing* is a priority," says Simon Fulleringer, Asset and Configuration Manager at McGill University. Or, as my dad used to say, "You can have anything you want – but you can't have everything you want." If you're in charge, learn to set priorities and be clear about them.

> *"That's why I'm the boss, and you're not."*

Comments like these tell everyone you might be the boss, but you're *not* a leader.

---

*"I shouldn't have to tell you you're doing a good job."*

---

Yes, you should.

A retiring Deputy Director with a large western city tells of a time when he took a moment to affix a sticky note to an annual performance review, giving the employee sincere thanks for doing an outstanding job. This Director was not actually delivering the review; he was approving it for a front-line supervisor to deliver to the employee.

Three years afterward, at an employee event, he was approached by the employee (whom he didn't actually know in person).

After introductions and small talk, the employee thanked him for writing the note (which the Director didn't even remember having written at this point). The employee went on to say, "I want you to understand how important that note was to me." He pulled out his wallet and showed the Director the note – which he had kept and carried for over three years.

People want to know – and deserve to know – when they're doing a good job. You may never know how important this can be.

---

*"I expect you to be on time for staff meetings." (Even if I'm consistently late.)*

---

If you're the manager, you're in the spotlight with your staff. All. The. Time. Famed psychiatrist Carl Jung once said, "It's not what you say that matters, it's what you do."

If you want people to come to meetings on time, *be there on time* yourself.

---

*"Sorry, but you'll just have to do more with less."*

---

This comment may be the most popular, but least useful, tired business-speak cliché. We can all do a little more with less if we're mindful of how we spend our time and energy. BUT let's be real – like rubber bands stretched too far, we'll snap. Here's how Pat Lynch, President of Business Alignment Strategies, Inc., put it:

"It's time to let go of the fantasy that we can do 'more with less.' Why? Because we can't – not if we're honest with ourselves. If we overburden people and systems, we will succeed only in burning out employees, experiencing equipment and process meltdowns, and cutting corners or engaging in other activities that will come back to haunt us in the long run – if not in the short run. Although it may seem counterintuitive, implementing a "doing less with less" strategy actually results in *increased* productivity and *decreased* stress.

"The new reality is NOT about doing more with less; it's about letting things go."

---

*"Please – leave your personal life at the door. You're here to work."*

---

Few of us like drama llamas. We all need to learn how to compartmentalize different spheres of life. It can be challenging for colleagues to stay focused on their work when a fellow employee is wallowing in a personal crisis.

That said, people are *not* machines, despite labels like "human resources" or "full-time equivalents." People bring skills, talent, *and* feelings and emotions to work. What happens at home does impact what happens at work – and vice versa.

Ineffective leaders are confused and alarmed when they see an employee struggling with a personal problem. They often don't know how to handle it. They often choose to ignore it, or tamp it down, or even insist that the employee snap out of it and focus on the job at hand.

Much better would be a strategy that includes:

- *Acknowledgement*: "You seem to be struggling with having to deal with caring for an aging parent."

- *Understanding*: "That's rough. It must be hard to find the best path forward."
- *Empathy*: "I think I might know a little about what you're going through. We had to put my mother in an assisted living place two years ago."
- *Assistance*. Perhaps, if the situation seems to warrant it, you can refer the employee to an Employee Assistance Program.

---

*"I'm in charge." (I don't have to justify or explain my decisions.)*

---

Au contraire! The best leaders are remarkably transparent. Perhaps this one should reframe the reaction he's getting. Perhaps he could say, "I'm in charge. Sometimes

I have to make difficult or unpopular decisions. Let me share some of what went into my thinking process." Employees recognize (and appreciate) that some decisions must be unilateral, made by the boss without any input, while others are improved through the active participation of staff.

They are far more likely to support decisions if they understand the process used to make them. If they don't, and they don't agree with a decision, they are more likely to sabotage that decision by second-guessing it, gossiping about it, or simply engaging in malicious compliance – meaning they'll carry it out to the letter of the directive, without applying any judgment when an obstacle arises. "The boss told me to do it like this. I know, in this instance, that's crazy. But the boss told me to do it like this."

## Sadly, the list of examples could go on and on

We could analyze many more:

- "Never talk to Jim without clearing it with me first."
- "You seem to forget who's most important around here." (Me)
- "If you don't like it here, you're free to leave."

What do ineffective leaders have in common when they're communicating? They're often:

- Demanding
- Demoralizing
- Demeaning

Furthermore, their communication is frequently:

- Top-down, rather than collegial
- One-way, rather than a dialogue
- Power-reinforcing, rather than empowering

Ω   Ω   Ω

*Everyone* can benefit from a focus on improving their communication. At times, we all deliver ineffective messages. A hallmark of the effective leader is the person who reflects from time to time on his or her messaging, with an aim toward reducing or eliminating those statements that do not encourage, understand, or acknowledge the importance of their employees.

The success of your communication lies in the *response* of the receiver. Period. It doesn't matter how well you think you said it. How the receiver reacts is what counts. If you're not getting the responses you want, it's not because the receiver "just doesn't get it." It's up to *you* to try another approach. Remember, as the saying goes, "If you keep on doing what you're doing, you'll keep on getting what you're getting."

## Chapter 14: Get Off Your But

Mary is headed back to her office with Ben, a new member of her team. He had given his first-ever status update at a project meeting. Mary feels he's done fairly well, with a clear command of the material. She is puzzled, however, at the number of questions meeting participants raised.

It occurs to her that some of the confusion could have been handled with handouts that expanded on the information Ben presented with PowerPoint charts and graphs. She decides this is a "coachable" moment where she could give him feedback on his performance.

She calls him into her office. She has two observations she wants to share:

1. Overall, the presentation went well, and

2. It could be improved next time with a few handouts

Like many of us, she's about to make a *big* completely unconscious mistake. She's going to sandwich the word "but" between the two thoughts. She's going to say, "That was a good presentation, Ben, *but* it would have been even more effective if you'd brought handouts to further clarify the slides."

C'mon now, what's wrong with that? Isn't it true?

It *is* true; it's specific; it's about behavior (which is critical when delivering performance feedback); it's certainly not rude. What's the problem?

It could have been delivered far more effectively, had she changed a single word. Compare this approach: "That was a good presentation, Ben, *and* it would have been even more effective if you'd brought handouts to further clarify the slides."

Do you see – and feel – the difference? It's so subtle, yet powerful. If you don't get it right away, try reading both comments again, out loud. Notice the difference in how they "land" on you.

What Mary may not realize is that while she can send a message around the world in a seventh of a second, it can take much longer to penetrate a quarter inch of human skull. She can improve her chances of getting through if she would use the word *and*.

Why?

Most people react to any statement that contains a "but" by discounting it and not believing it. When people say, "You did that well, *but* you could do this, too," all we hear is, "You didn't do that well."

"How do I look?" you say, before leaving for an important business dinner. Your friend says, "You look pretty good, *but* I'd wear a different shirt." You hear, "You don't look that good." The first half of the message is experienced as an attempt to "butter us up" before the shoe drops. You're more likely to believe the whole message if you heard, "You look pretty good, *and* I'd wear a different shirt."

While we're critiquing Mary's feedback to Ben, let's add something else. Using *and* is a marked improvement, but she could have been even more specific.

Oops! I should have said, "and she could do even better."

She could have said: "That presentation was quite effective, Ben. You had everyone's attention. I liked the way you sequenced the material, **and** I have one suggestion. Next time, you might consider having handouts for everyone to simplify the complicated points you were making."

Now she's even more specific about what she observed. She's told Ben exactly why she thought the presentation was good. The first half of her message has far more credibility now.

## Think I'm making too much of one little word?

Try it yourself. The next three times you have positive feedback that includes a suggestion to improve something, practice inserting the word *and* between the two thoughts. See whether the comment lands well.

Perhaps in the grand scheme of things, something as small as substituting *and* for *but* doesn't seem that important.

It is.

"Show me someone who cannot bother to do little things and I'll show you someone who cannot be trusted to do big things." Lawrence Bell, founder of Bell Aircraft Corporation

Or, as Peter Cohen, former CEO of Shearson Lehman Brothers, put it: "There is no one giant step that does it. It's a lot of little steps."

If the feedback is important enough to offer, it's important enough to deliver it so that it is heard and believed.

## But – but – but!

One more thing. *However* is just a three-syllable synonym for *but*. Don't try to finesse it. Just learn to make the substitution and you'll be far more effective sending your message. Remember, you're not manipulating the receiver. You're not fibbing. You're not sweet-coating the message. You're ensuring that it gets heard and completely believed.

Once you get in the habit of changing *but* to *and*, you will get your messages to smoothly penetrate that quarter inch of skull, and people will take your suggestions for improvement more readily.

It's hard to lead people if they don't believe half of what you're saying!

## Chapter 15: Sixteen Seconds of Silence

Keith was unhappy with the participation in his weekly staff meetings. His team was in crunch mode, under pressure to deliver, and he needed everyone on board. But when he would raise agenda items, his team rarely offered much input, and when they did, it was minimal. He couldn't decide whether there was fear or embarrassment – or something else – to blame for the situation.

Cindy dreaded her one-on-one meetings with Kyle. These scheduled events were supposed to be opportunities for each to debrief the other on how things were going, but she realized that most of the conversations were one-way affairs – she was doing most of the talking, and her questions were met with one-word answers.

Andy was a member of the Safety Committee, which met periodically to review incidents and responses. The gatherings were chaired by Phyllis, who had a reputation as a no-nonsense, action-oriented manager who wasn't particularly skilled or interested in building consensus. Questions were raised from time to time, but were met by silence or brief, non-committal responses.

There are many times when it can feel like pulling teeth to get someone to engage in a real conversation – an exchange of opinions and ideas. If you've found yourself stuck talking with someone and feeling like you're getting nowhere, this tip is for you.

# Leverage sixteen seconds of silence

Did you know that most of us can't tolerate more than about *sixteen seconds of silence* when an open-ended question has been asked?

"What's an open-ended question?" you might wonder.

Well, *that* was an open-ended question. Contrast it with:

"Do you know what an open-ended question is?"

Which is a closed-ended question.

Generally, open-ended questions can't be answered with a simple yes, no, okay, or "I'm good." Here are some examples:

- What resources will you need for this project?

- How will you have the report done by Friday?
- How did the issue between the two of you start?
- What do you plan to do when you've finished taking with Stephanie?
- How can I be helpful in this situation?

When you ask an open-ended question, a bit of tension is introduced into the conversation. The respondent feels a bit of pressure to say *something* more than a single word. If the question is closed-ended, such as:

- Do you agree with our new priorities?
- Are there merits to this proposal?

- Should we move the schedule up two weeks?

The respondent can eliminate the tension quite easily with a one- or two-word response:

- Sure
- Yeah
- Nope

"What obstacles do you imagine might derail this project?" – perfect open-ended question.

"Well, for one thing, the folks in Purchasing aren't likely to sign off on this." – useful answer.

"How so?" – terrific open-ended follow-up question!

Communication experts have established that when a bit of tension is introduced into a conversation, most of us can't tolerate more than about 16 seconds of silence before we feel compelled to say *something*.

Here's the tip in a single sentence: When you want to encourage participation in a conversation, ask an open-ended question. Then resist the temptation to answer your own question. You'll feel the same tension, and as those seconds tick along, you'll feel the impulse to reduce it yourself.

Manager to staffer: "Are there things we can do to respond more effectively to this issue?"

1 second…

2 seconds…

3 seconds…

4 seconds…

5 seconds…

6 seconds…

Manager then says: "For instance, should we send an all-hands memo?"

*Tension broken; silence ended.* Plus, it's a close-ended question.

Staffer: "Sure!"

Manager: "Sigh."

Instead, wait long enough, and you'll get something like this:

Staffer: "Well, it might help if there was a way to get everyone on the same page."

Manager: "Say more about that…"

Staffer: "Perhaps if we had a mandatory meeting for all staff. Or maybe just an email to everyone. Something like that…"

If they're not saying much, toss out an open-ended question. Then remain silent! Chances are, within 16 seconds or less, you'll get a response. The conversational ball has been nudged and is beginning to roll. Keith could do that at his staff meetings, Cindy could do that with Kyle, and Phyllis would help the Safety Committee reach genuine consensus if she laid the foundation for more robust dialogue.

# Chapter 16: Seriously – There Are Four Kinds of Truth?

Ray and Tracy are in the middle of an argument.

He's trying to explain why he didn't have all the numbers ready for Tracy by the deadline in the project schedule. Tracy reminds Ray he had plenty of time.

Ray tells her other things came up that demanded his attention.

Tracy responds by reminding Ray that getting those numbers was a top priority.

In short, the two are going 'round and 'round – and getting nowhere. Each is becoming entrenched in the belief that he or she is telling the truth.

The odd thing is they're both right.

## Old lady or young lady?

Consider the optical illusion you've seen many times. You see a face – but is it an old woman, looking down and to her left? Or is it a young woman, looking back over her right shoulder?

Yes. Both perceptions are correct and true – it depends on how you look at it.

A highly useful notion for anyone in a leadership role is that there may be *four* kinds of truth:

1. My truth – how I see a situation
2. Your truth – how you see a situation
3. Our truth – what we agree is the truth about a situation
4. The truth – the actual "real" truth (which might remain unknown to both of us)

Or, put another way:

1. I have my perception
2. You have your perception
3. We may agree on a mutual perception
4. But we may never know whether we've talked about the truth

Optical illusions can be fun. But when it comes to interpersonal conflict, not realizing when we're talking about different, equally compelling perceptions of the same circumstances can be debilitating.

"You never listen to my suggestions on how to do something!" is countered with...

"You never let me figure out things on my own!"

"But I'm trying to help!"

"You're not being helpful – you're meddling!"

and the digging in begins.

As leaders, we bear a little more responsibility to remind ourselves, and the people we're talking to, that there might be a perception issue clouding the actual issue. We need to own it when we realize we're presenting the facts as THE truth when it might be MY truth. A good leadership habit is to explore both (or every) side of an issue openly, planting your stake while being willing to move it. Look for common ground to discover OUR truth. Whether you get to THE truth is probably unknowable – and not particularly important anyway. Good leadership is helping people move from having sides to having common ground.

# Section Four: Offbeat and Unusual

This book, like its predecessor, is filled with tips, suggestions, techniques and ways about thinking about management every new leader should have when they got the promotion. And just like the first one, *What ELSE* has a couple of chapters that just didn't fit anywhere else.

- Did you know you can boost your effectiveness with fireflies?

- A tale about a finance manager who created a marvelous tool for team-building: T-shirts. Not what you might expect – free t-shirts for participants at an offsite event. Not even close.

## Chapter 17: What Do Fireflies Have to Do with It?

Have you ever been to Disneyland or Disneyworld? Ever ride the Pirates of the Caribbean? If so, you've seen one of Walt Disney's best-kept leadership secrets in action.

Remember how you boarded a long, flat boat at Lafitte's Landing? Then, after everyone was strapped in, off you went, swooshing into a dark lagoon set in the evening. It was an awesome depiction with incredible details: water, trees, mangroves, seagrasses, and even fireflies. Thousands of artificial fireflies. Of course, there were fireflies, right?

Did you know the attraction nearly opened with no fireflies whatsoever? At the time, no one realized the omission.

Go back to 1967, as the "imagineers," as they came to be called, were putting the finishing touches on the attraction. This was to be the last one that Disney personally helped design; it actually opened three months after his death.

After months of work, they were about to complete a final test ride and inspection by Disney and his aides. As the imagineers and their boss floated past the working restaurant known as The Blue Bayou, Walt suddenly shouted, "Stop!"

Someone pulled the brakes. "There's something wrong here. Something doesn't look right," said Disney, as the boat gently rocked.

They all stared at one another. No one could figure it out. What was wrong? Was something inaccurate? Was something malfunctioning? Had they overlooked anything? No one could say.

Then, someone remembered that there was a busboy working at The Blue Bayou who had grown up on the *real* bayou. He was located and brought to the scene. He was asked some version of "What's wrong with this picture?"

## It took him fifteen seconds.

"There's no fireflies!" he said. "If this was the real bayou, you'd have thousands of fireflies, flickering on and off everywhere."

Walt refused to have the attraction opened to the public until (legend has it) over 10,000 artificial fireflies were installed. And so it came to be.

Some say this is nothing more than a good example of Disney's eye for detail, but there's more than that. It's about a dynamic I call *fireflies*, which I define as details we can add to an experience that, if they were absent, might not be consciously missed. Hardly anyone would notice something that's not there. But once introduced, people would agree the experience was enhanced by those details – even if they couldn't tell you what they are.

Of the millions of people who have been on a boat on the Pirates of the Caribbean, most have never been to a real bayou. The might not realize there were supposed to be fireflies. But, if asked, all would agree that having 10,000 artificial fireflies really completed the scene.

## A few more examples

A colleague and fellow consultant tells the story of a time when he was asked to facilitate a transition workshop for a new manager. The manager's administrative assistant, Stephanie, asked how he wanted the room arranged. Among other things, my colleague asked if she could make some name tents for each participant to put on the tables.

He arrived at the session expecting something simple – perhaps some cardstock folded over with the names printed by hand using a marker. It would certainly have been sufficient.

Stephanie took it a couple of steps further by adding some "fireflies" to the name tents. She'd personalized each one for its owner by adding some artwork that reflected something about their interests or personality. Everyone at the workshop was delighted with their name tents – and they all saved them as a memento of the experience. When's the last time you saved your name tent from a seminar? Those were fireflies.

## Here's another

I was in Chicago to work with a new client. At the airport, I climbed into a cab. I was in for a shock – on the back seat were three freshly folded newspapers – *The Wall Street Journal*, the *Chicago Tribune*, and the *Chicago Sun Times* – provided for passengers to read. What's more, the cab smelled fresh – unlike like most cabs I've taken. The driver was upbeat but not intrusive.

When I arrived at my destination, the cabbie asked if I'd be needing another cab to return to the airport. Of course I would! He gave me his card, and, believe me – I called him when I needed that cab.

If those newspapers hadn't been available on the back seat, I would not have noticed. They weren't expected and wouldn't have been missed. But they were there – *fireflies* in a cab.

## One more

A leader I greatly admire has long practiced a true *firefly* habit. Early in any new professional relationship (with staff, clients, or colleagues) she learns their birthdate. She travels around the world, and she began to bring a stack of cards with her. To pass the time, she would write a note – a thank you, a "thinking of you," or a birthday message to all her contacts. She mails them when she arrives at her destination.

Once she began hearing back from her colleagues about how much they appreciated getting these notes, she made it a habit.

It's a gesture that survives an earlier time when people corresponded with hand-written messages. In an era of email, text messages, voice mail, and Skype, these personalized notes are far more appreciated by everyone who gets one. Does she *have* to send personal notes to keep in contact with her network? Obviously, no – and most of us don't. But I'd warrant her fireflies have helped her build a stronger, more loyal network than most.

Fireflies are really "small stuff." They may be little things, but they can make a huge impact.

Ask yourself: What fireflies can you add to your leadership practice?

## Chapter 18: Team Building with Tee Shirts

One day, I was working with a finance manager one day and watched him step *far* "outside the box" to invent a clever new way to elevate his team's performance.

He'd assembled the group for a meeting. Once it began, he told them he had something he wanted to talk about – something that wasn't on the agenda. He sounded serious; the room got quiet. Phil began telling them that he'd been reflecting about how to take this team "to the next level." He said he was wondering whether there were little things that could be done that would make a big difference.

"One thing I realized," he said, "is that I interrupt you in these meetings far too often. Sometimes I get so excited about *my* idea that I don't really take the time to listen to yours.

But I don't like that I do that. It's rude and unfair to you."

Then, he said, "I'm going to change that."

The people around the conference table said nothing. You probably know what they were thinking, right? *Sure…he says that, but will he follow through?* Or perhaps, *It's about time!*

Phil stood up and went on to say, "I really mean what I'm saying. I'm making a full commitment to cut my interruptions to a minimum." As the group watched, Phil took off his jacket, removed his tie, and began unbuttoning his shirt. The group stared as Phil then removed his shirt, revealing a tee shirt he'd had made at a shirt shop for this occasion. On the front was printed, "I will not interrupt my team!"

Everyone chuckled, and then Phil took it another step. What he'd done was already good theatre, perhaps, but his next act took his leadership up a notch. He passed out a one-page handout to each person. On the sheet of paper was a drawing of the outline of a tee shirt.

"Now," he said, "I want you to think about one thing *you* could do differently that could help raise our team to even better performance. It's not just my responsibility – we are one team, and we all share the responsibility. Think about it – what could you do to help this team improve, if you chose to do it? Write it down on that handout."

For the next few minutes, people reflected and then scribbled something on their handout. Phil asked them to share what they'd written. The ideas were simple yet profound.

> - *I could come to meetings better prepared.*

- *I could stop trying to prevail in every conversation.*
- *I could bury the hatchet with Jim and move on.*
- *I could speak up more often.*

Around the table they went, as each person shared what he or she could do to help make the team more effective.

When they were finished, Phil simply said, "We all know what we could do. Now, let's just do it."

Ω    Ω    Ω

You know what? That's exactly what they did. It's pretty hard to declare in public what you could do differently and then not do it.

Afterwards, I teased Phil a bit. "You know what you've just done? You've pulled off a full-blown team building in fifteen minutes."

Phil couldn't have been happier with the results.

# Afterword

We've come to the end of the *What Your Boss Never Told You* journey. It's been such a pleasure to share insights, tips and techniques for the new(er) manager that I've learned over my career. If I've made you more aware, made you think, and perhaps even made you laugh along the way, I've done what I've set out to do.

There are many things your boss may not have thought to tell you when you made your transition from worker bee to the person in charge.

We've explored the skills you'll need to succeed – technical, political and interpersonal.

We covered a variety of practical communication tips, from examples of what effective leaders say (and what they *shouldn't* say), to considering saying "and" instead of "but" and using 16 seconds of silence to encourage others to comment.

You should feel better equipped to make better decisions, knowing when to involve your staff and when to make them on your own, and how to reach consensus without beating a dead horse. You've seen tips on how to run more effective meetings.

You should have a good idea what your X-Factor is, how to foster loyalty, and even how to use fireflies to take your leadership practice to a higher level. You may know more about how to motivate others than most managers with years of experience.

We've considered how to give people a compelling sense of purpose – it's all about the Kool Aid, remember? And you now know that one of the most important things you can give your people is the experience of being heard.

Now you're better equipped to resolve dilemmas that rise when you must choose between doing things according to "the book," and doing what you know is the right thing to do. With the chapters that unpacked motivation, you know more about how to get the best from your staff than most managers know with years of experience.

Leading others as their supervisor or manager is not easy. It can be complicated, challenging and quite rewarding. You get to make a difference. You touch lives. You can inspire others to achieve their potential.

I'll leave you with one more tip. If you *really* want to learn anything from this book, or from your next management seminar, or from a Ted Talk, *teach* it to someone else. Here's how Loris Malaguzzi, an early childhood education specialist once put it:

"Learning and teaching should not stand on opposite banks and just watch the river flow by, they should embark together on a journey down the water. Teaching strengthens how much one learns."

Ω   Ω   Ω

Take time to *enjoy* your leadership experience. Amidst all the issues, the achievements and the setbacks, remember to hit the pause button every now and then and simply appreciate the gifts and opportunity you've been given. At the end of the day,

"If your actions inspire others to dream more, learn more, do more, and become more, you are a leader."

Bon voyage!

# About the author

Gary Winters has consulted with leaders in over 300 organizations, including high tech manufacturing, hospitals, schools, cities, counties, state and federal agencies, water districts, and public boards and commissions. He is past president of the Organization Development Network of San Diego and former director of the Management Development Center at San Diego State University.

He is the creator of The Leadership Almanac, a blog which explores the practical side of leadership with articles ranging from how leaders create a compelling vision to how they sweat the small stuff, from how they make tough decisions to how they navigate a difficult conversation, from how they inspire to what makes them perspire.

He is the author of six books:

*What Your Boss Never Told You – A Quick Start Guide for New Managers*

*What ELSE Your Boss Never Told You – More Timely Tips for New Managers*

*To Do or Not To Do – How Successful Leaders Make Better Decisions*

*Managing Friends and Former Peers*

*Managing Friends & Former Peers*

*Managing the Soon-to-Retire Employee*

*So, How Was Your Meeting?*

As a consultant, Gary specializes in:

- Executive coaching
- Leadership seminars / workshops / retreats
- Team building

Home-based in Reno, Nevada, he works with clients throughout the United States. His personal interests include photography, recumbent trike cycling, and music (currently, he's taking lessons on the mountain dulcimer.)

www.ingramcontent.com/pod-product-compliance
Lightning Source LLC
Chambersburg PA
CBHW052144220526
45471CB00004B/1525